Table of Contents

Feel Good

Formula

Change Your Mood,
Change Your Mind,
Change Your Life

Roger Steward

Introduction

"How are you feeling?"

This is a question we tend to get asked a lot. But how do you find yourself typically responding to this type of question? Most of the time you may answer with a quick, "fine," or "good," without really giving it a second thought. It's become an instant reflex to say that you're doing fine that you've nearly forgotten what it means to feel fine or good. What's shocking is that you may even say these things when, in actuality, you feel like you're on the brink of having a complete internal meltdown.

We've all experienced general unhappiness throughout our lives, in a constant state of just being "fine". But do we ever tell people the truth about how we're feeling? Not really. What's worse is that most of the time we don't even tell ourselves that we're feeling bad. We instead cling to those feelings, which harm us instead of help us. We don't typically deal with these feelings and instead bury them deep down to never see the light of day. When this happens, it can severely affect the moods we're in.

Since the world is constantly changing, we strive (and struggle) to keep up with how fast it's moving. We live such busy lives from the moment we wake up to the moment our head hits the pillow at the end of the day. But all that moving and changing keeps us locked into the same habits and patterns, a routine that we soon find unsatisfying. This routine takes a toll on us, and soon we find ourselves feeling "off" or in a "funk" as some people call it. We drift through the rest of the day lost in the traffic of our thoughts while we complete tasks we'll hardly remember doing later on.

When we're lacking awareness and positive thinking, life just seems a little more difficult. It's harder to get up in the morning. We grow disgruntled with our jobs, classes, and even the hobbies we used to enjoy. We tend to ignore the things we are grateful for, and often forget how good we have it if we're too focused on all the bad things in our lives. All of these can stew into the perfect recipe for a terrible mood.

But life doesn't always have to be this way. Don't you wish there was a way to stop your negative thoughts and emotions from controlling you? Wouldn't you like to have a day where you're not stuck in a bad mood? You just want to know what it's like to feel good again. You want to be fulfilled. By shifting your way of thinking, and taking the time to understand your moods and how they affect you, you can have all of the above!

In this book, you'll be getting a crash course on gaining a better perspective to change your mind, change your mood, and change your life! These chapters that follow will cover what moods are, the differences between positive and negative moods, and how to recognize and understand moods as they come. You'll learn how to change your moods by restructuring your outlook on life and how you view others. Finally, these chapters will also explain a wide range of tools to choose from and practice with, such as mindfulness, meditation, and maintaining a healthy lifestyle to keep your moods in check. By the time you finish this book, instead of brushing off your feelings and labeling them as "fine," you should be asking yourself, "How am I feeling...*really*?" Through recognizing and growing familiar with changes to your mood, you will put yourself on the successful path of living a fulfilling and happy life!

Chapter One

Understanding Your Moods

"Sorry, I'm just a little moody today." Have you ever heard yourself say some variation of this phrase? Typically we're referring to having a bad day when we say this. But what does it really mean to feel "moody?" In actuality, our moods aren't always necessarily bad, and sometimes they're even surprisingly complex to narrow down to "good" and "bad".

Our moods function a lot like houseguests. Good houseguests provide you with a good time, and you don't seem to mind when they stick around. You want them to stay because you're having such a good time with them. You feel like you go about your day without any issues arising between the two of you. But other times certain guests tend to show up unannounced and uninvited. These guests are more rude and exhausting when you have to keep up with them. They disrupt your schedule and don't have any respect for your 'house,' whenever they stay. Even when you try to kick them out, they put up a fight when it's time to leave. The longer they stay, the more it takes a toll on you, and you'll soon suffer because of it.

But you don't want to suffer anymore. Instead, you want to focus on feeling good. This means that you'll need to equip yourself with the right tools and ways of thinking that'll help you be happy again. With your newfound strength, you'll soon feel like we have the power to turn away those unwanted houseguests before they can even knock on your door.

In this chapter we'll be talking all about moods: explaining what they are, how they come about through our environment, how they're related to emotions, as well as focusing on how to recognize, monitor, understand, and change your moods for the better.

What is a Mood?

The most basic dictionary definition of the word "mood" means a temporary state of mind or feeling. Moods are that feeling we get when everything seems to be going just right in our lives. But with good days also come the bad ones. Moods also make us feel like we want to give up, crawling back into bed to sulk. They can be happy, content, sad, angry, frustrated, and anxious. It's also up to us to change them when they're overstaying their welcome.

Like our emotions, moods are typically triggered by events or experiences we have. When you do something that you truly enjoy, how do you tend to feel for the rest of the day? Great, right? How about when you fight with your friend or significant other? Now you're feeling not so great...

Our moods exist in a couple of ways: Voluntarily and involuntarily. We can achieve them through the things we enjoy doing. Sometimes we're able to purposely seek out hobbies or activities that put us in a good mood afterward. But sometimes they can also get out of hand and arrive without warning, like unexpected (and unwanted) houseguests. When this happens, the mood is a little more difficult to shake off. But we shouldn't be afraid of bad moods when they arrive. It's much better to feel out your moods and study them to not make them seem as ominous. Moods are a sort of "template," or guide for how our day is going to go. Depending on the mood, we can experience entirely different ranges of feelings throughout the day in an intricate cycle.

But Wait! Are Moods and Emotions The Same?

There's often plenty of debate between the two because they seem so similar. Both moods and emotions relate to how we feel, but they are certainly not the same thing.

The main difference between the two is the length of time in which they are felt. In Dr. Paul Ekman's book, "Emotions Revealed," he discusses that moods last for an extended period of time, at least for a couple of days. He also says that moods are generally emotional feelings. This can seem a little confusing since all three of those words sounds like the same thing. But we can break it down a little more than that: A mood impacts our emotions like a chain reaction. You experience a rush of different emotions, which are then built up to create a mood that's either positive or negative.

Moods and emotions tend to work in tandem as a complex system of feelings. Think about when you feel in a "good mood." You're much kinder to the people around you. You're more compelled to be productive and feel completely at ease. By being in a good mood, you're more likely to express your emotions positively. We smile more, laugh more, and overall we enjoy life more.

But it's also not always sunshine and rainbows for us. Our bad moods bring out emotions of discontent, annoyance, and frustration. We may be more likely to grow impatient with others, even throw out a rude comment at someone depending on the situation. Emotions are "hot" like little sparks that burn bright but fizzle out. They're usually expressed only temporarily, and yet we experience hundreds if not thousands of them per day. Circumstances like conversations or memories tend to trigger our emotions rather than our moods. You may grow excited seeing a dog walking past you on the sidewalk, but only for that fleeting moment. A mood is a feeling you wake up with, go about your day with, and eventually go to sleep with, depending on how long the mood lasts.

What Also Impacts Our Moods?

We may be surprised to realize that our moods stick around a little longer than we think, and part of it can be caused by the way we live and react to the world around us. There are plenty of environmental factors involved that can contribute to how your moods are brought out. Many of them relate to long-term conditions in our lives such as work or home life. Here are some of the most common examples of everyday situations that impact our moods.

- Stress: Do you seem to constantly have a lot on your plate? Are you busy with work, school, or your home? When you are stressed or are often in the middle of stressful situations, it's easier to become overwhelmed by everything we have to do, especially when we allow it to be our main focus.

- Sleeping Patterns: Are you getting enough sleep? Sleep is such a crucial function for our bodies, with hundreds of benefits that include healing your body and your mind while. Your brain depends on its rest to function properly throughout the day. Depending on how much sleep you get, you may experience feeling either well-rested or irritable, which can influence your mood for the day.

- Human Interactions: Spending time with friends and family can put us in a great mood, especially when we're having fun and building positive memories with those people. But if we have an unpleasant encounter with someone at work, home, running errands, or at school, we may spend the rest of the day feeling terrible. It's especially effective on our moods if our daily activities require us to work with people we don't get along with.

- Your Living Environment: How and where you live plays a huge role in your mood. Having a messy house can take away the sense of comfort a home is supposed to provide. With clutter around your house, it can become more difficult to focus, especially when you're always worrying about the mess. You may have to live with a family that doesn't get along, which can cause a negative association with your home. You may also live in a noisy or unsafe neighborhood, which can increase your levels of stress and impact your sleep, which then affects your mood. A clean house can make you feel calmer, and of living in a safe place can also put your mind at ease.

- <u>Drugs and Alcohol:</u> Drugs and Alcohol are notorious for changing moods. What can make these substances more dangerous is when someone uses them to change his or her mood when they're feeling down. This creates a dependence on these substances, and the next time you feel bad you'll reach for these things to make you feel better. This behavior can make moods much worse. Alcohol is a depressant, which slows down your body and your brain functions so that you can't think as clearly. As a result of using these substances frequently, you're putting yourself at risk from making good decisions. Since they are mind-altering you're also clouding your brain from healthily processing your feelings.

- <u>Poor Diet</u>: We'll be taking a closer look at this factor in chapter five, but the way you eat can affect the way you feel throughout the day. Ever notice when you eat a lot of bread or pasta you find yourself getting tired midway through the day? Some foods can make us drowsy or energized. Some people may enjoy the effects of caffeine, which is known for boosting energy, but too much of it can make you irritated or make you crash later in the day. The more healthy choices you make, the more likely you'll feel balanced and in a good mood.

While our lifestyle and our environment are more known for affecting our moods, some factors may seem more out of our control:

- Seasons/Weather: Depending on your preference, the weather can set the tone for your day. We tend to lean towards more depressive tendencies when it's cold or raining outside. When the sun is shining, we sometimes feel like we're shining with it. If it's too hot, though, we could feel lethargic and not want to go outside.

- Hormonal Changes: Hormones affect our brains in a variety of ways. If your body is going through changes, you may experience an adverse reaction in your moods. Women who are pregnant are known for experiencing highly unpleasant moods, often feeling tired and irritated as their hormones fluctuate. Other examples include menstrual cycles and menopause that also play a role in experiencing drastic mood swings.

- Mental Illness: Depression and Anxiety can be developed over time, but also having a chemical imbalance can lead to some people developing these mental illnesses later on. Your brain chemistry can impact your mood if not treated by a medical professional. Environment can also play a part in those who have anxiety, depression, ADHD, and other mental illnesses. It's important to seek outside help if experiencing negative moods for extended periods of time.

- World News: With so much access to technology, and being able to access worlds of information at our fingertips, it's sometimes hard to get away from what's going on in the world. It can be discouraging to us when we see that negative events are constantly happening all over the world. It seems like every day something is going wrong, things we would never want to happen. We may feel scared, frustrated, or even helpless to know there are things far from our control. It's okay to feel a sense of hurt for others in the world, but it can take a toll on us mentally when we exert all of our energy into world events.

Monitoring Your Moods

Data is essential to learn new information. By keeping track of an event, you're more likely to see patterns and cause-and-effect reactions that form because of that event. So how does this apply to moods? Why should you monitor them? By keeping track of your moods, you're creating a better understanding of yourself and how your mind reacts to situations. By studying how you feel over a length of time, you'll notice the patterns will start to emerge. You may find out you were more stressed because you had a big project at work for the past few days. Your good mood might be a result of the weekend getaway you had planned during the month. By keeping tabs on your moods, the next time you find yourself in a tense situation or are just feeling down, you'll be able to understand how and why you felt the way you did once you're feeling better.

Because they stick with us longer than emotions, sometimes moods are persistent and hard for us to get out of. One of the main reasons it's difficult for us is because when we're in a bad or complicated mood, it becomes harder for us to see our lives in a more positive light. If a negative mood lasts for a few days, we may start to believe that our lives have always been this negative. It can be scary to think, "I've always been miserable and always will be." That's the exact opposite of wanting to change our lives for the better. We allow negative moods to overcome us, so much that we don't realize we're missing out on all of the good things that are actually in our lives…sometimes right in front of us!

With that frame of thinking, you quickly bubble up with the negative emotions associated with our bad mood. You might even be frustrated to find that you've gotten stuck in a particular mood for longer than you had thought. Soon it all comes to a full boil. You lash out at your friends and family without thinking, or you resort to reclusive behavior altogether. This is where moods can be dangerous if not dealt with properly.

By monitoring your moods, you'll discover that you can manage your feelings better, and allow yourself to feel good quickly. It becomes easier to understand why you're feeling positive or negative feelings, and how they all connect back to what your mood is at the time. Your life will be healthier because you will have a better sense of yourself and make better decisions, which in turn will improve your overall wellbeing.

There are plenty of resources to help you keep tabs on how you've been feeling, but one of the simplest ways to do so is by using a mood tracker. Mood trackers exist online, but you can also draw up a quick one on a sheet of paper, in a journal, or on a calendar. It can be as serious or as fun as you'd like to make it. A popular way to track moods is a drawn-up calendar with certain colors associated with certain moods. You can write down your mood in a journal, along with a short description of your day that includes positive times, negative times, and times where you felt your emotions the strongest.

When tracking your mood, it's best to keep an eye on the highest and lowest points of how you're feeling. Try to notice when your mood is fluctuating, and record how you feel in those moments. It also helps to keep track of your daily habits to help you better understand why you were feeling those moods. Things like sleeping habits, diet, and workload can all be tracked as well.

To give you a full scope of your moods, it's a good idea to keep tabs for a few weeks, even a month or two. The more you practice this exercise, the more you'll be able to make connections between your habits and your changing moods. Your tracker might also help you see things from a new, more positive perspective. When you see that not every single day you have is a bad day, it helps reframe your thinking that moods are not necessarily permanent. Conversely, if you've noticed that your moods have been bad for several days, maybe it's time to consider taking a day to recover and try to do something to help alleviate your stress.

What to Look For:

While monitoring your moods, in times that you can't record them, it's also helpful to mentally keep tabs on your emotions while they happen, so that you have better control over them. We'll be covering how to be mindful about emotions and thoughts in the next chapter, and how to deal with negative ones. For starters, though, you can monitor how your negative and positive emotions affect your body. If you feel a particularly strong emotion, you can track how it made you felt that day to help you understand your changing moods.

Here are some negative emotions to look for, and some ways they might feel:

- Anger: frustrated, irritated, grouchy, a tightened facial expression, tense-feeling body, wanting to lash out or 'attack' by shouting or raising your voice.
- Envy: longing, bitter, unsatisfied with what you have, thinking you don't have something as good as someone else, not feeling like you have enough
- Disgust: 'grossed-out,' annoyed, displeased, feeling nauseous, feeling like you're 'dirty' or 'unclean' or that you need to cleanse yourself, not wanting the offensive person or object to be near you
- Fear: uncomfortable, pounding heart, heavy breathing, sweaty palms, feeling on-edge, scared, anxious, panicked, wanting to run or hide somewhere, wanting to retreat away from others or unpleasant situations
- Jealousy: intense guarding over someone or something, feeling unwanted or not needed by someone close to you,

fear of losing something, feeling angry or inadequate when jealous of others

- <u>Shame:</u> embarrassed, shy, warm face or increased body temperature, not wanting to look at others or have them look at you, feeling like you have to apologize, treading lightly when talking
- <u>Sadness:</u> hopelessness, a 'low' feeling, an emptiness, wanting to cry or yell, experiencing tiredness or low energy, wanting to give up, thinking there's no point to anything
- <u>Guilt:</u> can go hand-in-hand with feelings of shame, regretful, pit in your stomach, wanting to apologize, feeling at fault for something, nervousness, desperately hoping to change something for the better, practicing other options in your mind you wish you could have done

There are several negative emotions to look for when in a bad mood. But even in darker times, there are still some positive emotions to look for when they happen:

- <u>Happiness:</u> light, cheerful, excited, wanting to smile, an overall sense of positivity, wanting to do good things for yourself and others
- <u>Love:</u> excited, feeling close emotionally, wanting to be around someone or something you enjoy, selflessness, warm and joyful
- <u>Content:</u> deep satisfaction with your environment, not wanting anything but what you have at the moment, comfortable, relaxed, feeling like you have nothing to complain about

The Ego

Emotions and moods are necessary for us as people. We can dive even deeper than the outside factors in our lives to understand where our moods come from. Sometimes, the cause of bad moods comes from something that has resided within us from the time we were young. From a psychological standpoint, if we want to pursue true happiness, we first need to recognize a huge adversary that lives right inside our minds: Our ego.

Neurologist and father of psychoanalysis, Sigmund Freud, created a structural model that explains the purpose of our ego. It's one of three parts that makes up a personality. In the most basic sense, the ego is how we perceive ourselves. It's made up of all the information that makes you...*you*, like where you came from and your likes and dislikes. We usually like to think that we have a clear sense of ourselves. But have you ever had that little voice in the back of your mind? You know, the one that always tells you you're not good enough or points out your flaws? This is your ego, and it loves to talk. Unfortunately, it doesn't always have something nice to say to you.

And yet, we still find ourselves listening to it, and quite a lot of the time. Throughout the day, we have so many negative thoughts and critiques of ourselves. It's hard to push them away sometimes, and can often sound something like this:

"I'm so ugly."
"I'm not smart enough to know how to do this."
"I'm so bad at [insert anything here] and I'll never get the hang of it."

These are only some of the lies our ego tells us. It's so easy to believe them too because we connect phrases like this to ourselves and take these statements as if they were true. In reality, the mind is a complicated thing. It's tricky a lot of times because we have millions of thoughts throughout the day that we forget how important it is to be more aware of them. Just because you have a thought about something doesn't necessarily mean it's the truth.

The ego can get in our way of trying to achieve happiness in our lives. It makes us feel like we have to live up to a certain set of standards. Instead of enjoying life around us, we're too busy worrying about what the ego has to say about us. We're reminded of past mistakes and insecurities that it prevents us from wanting to branch out from our comfort zone because we're too afraid. But the truth is, we were the ones that drew up those standards in the first place. And just as easily as we created them, we have the power to completely change how we perceive ourselves, which will be explored in the next few chapters. As you read on, keep in mind of your ego, what it tells you now and how you'd like to form your perceptions of yourself for the better.

Chapter Two

The Power of Now

Your mind is very powerful and has the potential for you to be your very best. But sometimes we have trouble unlocking that potential when we're holed up in our minds, turning on our "Brain TV." Imagine your brain as if all your thoughts, memories, experiences, and emotions were channels on a television. Now, instead of enjoying the beauty of the world around you and paying attention to the small details in your life, you may find yourself busy flipping through these channels.

You watch where a thought leads for a while, and wait to see what the next "show" will be, and the next. Some are just simple thoughts, like what you're going to make for dinner or your plans for the day ahead. Your Brain TV may also cycle through more stressful channels, such as unpleasant experiences in your life, or how you should have said something different in a recent conversation.

Much like actual television, when you continue to watch these channels, you tend to zone out and ignore the world around you. You stare at the screen, replaying thoughts or worries over and over. Sometimes you get so lost in them, that when you finally tune out of your Brain TV, you can hardly remember what you were doing before or how long you were watching it in the first place. Not only can this make you tired, but it can also upsetting when you realize you've missed out on something exciting or worthwhile happening right in front of you. Lifelong memories are waiting to be created, and they don't need to be tainted with things that no longer matter in your life.

The thoughts you spend time with can certainly affect your moods. If your Brain TV is endlessly flipping through channels of unfortunate times in your life, they'll bring up a lot of negative emotions like guilt, shame, fear, or anger. Even though there's no way to completely shut off your Brain TV, there's certainly a way to keep yourself from tuning into it all day, and at least be able to lower the volume so it's playing in the background.

One of the most important skills you can polish to help you change your mood and make you feel good again is mindfulness. Now that we know about what moods and emotions are, what can we learn when it comes to changing them? There are a wide variety of ways to change your mood, and one of the biggest methods of improving your moods is to make the change from the inside out.

This chapter will help you understand how your mind and your emotions shape your moods. It will also cover how to use mindfulness and understand actual concepts used in behavioral therapy to change your moods. You'll learn to utilize these concepts to unlock the highly sought after, "Wise Mind," which helps tune out your Brain TV when it's at its loudest.

What is Mindfulness?

Echkard Tolle, a spiritual teacher and author of the book, *The Power of Now*, illustrates how your mind influences the way you live your life: "The mind is a superb instrument if used rightly. Used wrongly, however, it becomes very destructive. To put it more accurately, it is not so much that you use your mind wrongly—you usually don't use it at all. It uses you."

To further examine Tolle's idea of how the mind works, picture this scenario: You are spending time with someone, a friend or significant other. Perhaps you're walking down the sidewalk together as they talk to you. You'd like to think you were listening, but your brain is taking you on a trip elsewhere.

"It's really hot outside today, maybe I should buy a fan for my room. When was the last time I cleaned my room? Last week? Speaking of cleaning, I need to pick up some new sponges, maybe some things to put together for dinner too. Pasta? No, I had that yesterday. It was when my friend was over. There were so many messy dishes… They probably thought my house was so disgusting. They probably think I'm disgusting. They wouldn't think that, would they? Does this person I'm talking to think I'm disgusting? Maybe if I wasn't so lazy I could-"

You look over, only to find your friend has been waiting for an answer from you for a while…but to what question? You would know if you had only been listening and being mindful!

Mindfulness, in its simplest term, is a state of awareness. It means paying attention to your surroundings and the sensations you feel from them, rather than staying tucked away in your mind. Through this practice, you're more likely to feel 'in the moment' and savor the things you might have been missing out on. Mindfulness is about really enjoying what's in front of you, and using your senses as a guide to remind you that right here…right now, you are living, breathing, and alive.

Where are you now as you read this book? What do you see around you? What does your body feel like wherever you're sitting? Are you in the comfort of your home, in a busy café, or on your commute? What sounds can you hear? Any interesting smells? Are you enjoying a snack or a drink as you read? If so, how does it taste? All of these questions pertain to living a life of mindfulness. It's a connection you share with the universe around you, allowing yourself to be a part of it rather than fighting against it.

How many times have you been doing something that you enjoy, only to realize that instead of living in the moment you were too caught up in your thoughts? You might realize that you haven't been paying as much attention in your life as you had thought. A lot of truth can be found in Tolle's words, him being an avid practitioner of mindfulness.

We live in a world of distractions, ones that have made us unhappy as a result. You have a right to your happiness and to understand how your mind works in order to achieve said happiness. Most of the time, though, we allow our minds to think as they please. We also accept most of our thoughts without a second glance, or without realizing we're walking around an endless path in our heads.

To learn how to be mindful, it's important to recognize the places our thoughts tend to drift toward the most, the past and the future. We remember the past because it contains all of our life experiences. It serves as our base for learning and growing, as well as the memories we like to look back on. We think of the future because it's a vision of us ahead of our time. The future provides us with something to look forward to and shape ourselves towards. Our goals are in the future, so are our hopes and dreams. There's nothing wrong with reminiscing on pleasant memories or getting excited about future plans. However, it becomes a problem when we spend too much time in these moments, especially when we concentrate on the negative aspects of them. The past often plagues us with bad memories and regrets, while the future can fill us with haunting worries of what we'll never know will happen.

But in between the past and future, there's another element of time we can truly put our focus in: The Present. The present is everything that is happening to you right now, and it's crucial to achieving personal happiness. Why? Because it's the only place we actually have the most power

No matter how we try to justify it, anything from your past doesn't exist anymore because it's in the past, locked in, already happened. You will never, ever be able to go back and change anything from it. The future doesn't even exist either because it's not even *here* yet. There's no way for you to get a clear glimpse of the future, other than your predictions (which aren't reliable either) Since it's always capable of changing, you will truly never know what the future will bring. That sounds scary, right? After all, how can we NOT look back or ahead? What if the key to our happiness was a few steps back or it's somewhere waiting for us at the end? What if we miss something important?

Here's your answer: You won't. Because the past and future only exist in your mind, practically made up of memories and speculations. So, why waste time trying to figure them out? The important things you are missing are the tangible things in front of you at this moment. That is what makes the present so beautiful. It's the only moment in time that you can control: now, and now, and even right now! The present doesn't care about the embarrassing mistakes or regrets from a long time ago, nor does it worry about what's going to happen to us in the future.

But how can we keep ourselves in the present? Through mindfulness, of course! Mindfulness keeps you glued to what's happening NOW, and anytime you find yourself drifting away from the present, you can use mindfulness to bring yourself right back.

What are the Benefits of Mindfulness?

Mindfulness carries a plethora of positive effects on our mental health and moods. The most beneficial effect is that it allows you to be more in control of your mind, rather than it controlling you 24/7. You'll have more power to shape your thoughts and emotions and deal with unpleasant experiences with finesse. Along with this, practicing mindfulness can also decrease your feelings of suffering and instead boost your happiness. Here are some other benefits that mindfulness provides:

You'll Have a Clearer Mind – have you ever felt like you had so much going on during the day that your brain felt 'heavy' by the time your day was over? By practicing mindfulness for even a few minutes a day, you're giving your brain time to actually "breathe." It's exhausting to keep thinking, and soon you may start to realize it takes a toll on the rest of your body as well. A lot of times you might be thinking about the huge and never-ending list of things you need to accomplish during your day and even the day after that. Staying mindful temporarily takes you out of your mind, and instead puts your focus on something tangible and real.

You're Truly Experiencing Reality – Too often, your body carries you through the day without you really thinking. We've "programmed" ourselves with daily patterns and rituals, and have done them for so long we can do them without thinking. We go to the store and back home without even remembering the drive we took. Our minds wander during these times, as they often like to do. Before you know it, it's the end of the day and you're back in bed already forgetting everything you have accomplished. Mindfulness makes life more vivid and real, something you can experience instead of just wandering through. You'll feel like you're a part of this world, functioning with it, not outside it. You'll also feel more fulfilled when you take the time to look around and take a moment to appreciate the gift that life has to offer.

You'll be More Relaxed – Mindfulness also means being more aware of your moods. When you're focused on the moment, you're more likely to sense what feelings are going on inside as you feel them. Also, when you keep your mind in the present you're less likely to worry about the past or the future, things that can't affect your worries anymore. It takes an enormous weight off of your shoulders and is extremely comforting to know that what matters is the 'now,' and the best you can do is really appreciate it for what it is.

A Quick Mindful Exercise

A common exercise to practice mindfulness includes using all of your senses to learn information and to learn how to be in the present. Find something small in your house you can eat like a cracker, a piece of candy, or a peanut. Hold it in your hand, but don't eat it just yet! Instead, you'll be using your senses to see what you can learn from it.

- Look: What does it look like? What color is your object? Does it have any distinctive markings you notice? How about its shape? Is it round, bumpy, or a square?
- Feel: Does the object have a smooth or rough surface? Does it squish in your fingers, or is it firm? Is it light or have a little weight to it?
- Smell: Give it a whiff. Is there anything you notice about the smell? Even if it doesn't have one, you can maybe smell hand soap or lotion on your hands.
- Hear: This one might feel especially silly to do, but hold the object to your ear and listen to how it sounds between your fingers. Maybe it doesn't sound like much, but still, try to pay attention if it makes any kind of sound.
- Taste: Okay, now you can eat it! But do it slowly, really focusing on the flavor and texture on your tongue. Does it feel a certain way against your teeth as you chew? Does it make a crunch? Is it salty or sweet, or even both? Can you catch any distinct flavors that may be in it?
  Once you've done this exercise, take a moment to think about how it made you feel. Did it feel good to just practice a small bit of mindfulness? Even for a moment, you've forgotten about the channels changing in your Brain TV and tuned in to reality.

Slowing Down

Too often we try to rush through life to get things done. This only makes us unhappy because we're not paying attention to the experiences that life provides, even if it's during the most mundane activities. Do things slowly and with purpose. When practicing mindfulness, focus on being much slower than you normally would to give you enough time to be mindful about what you're doing. Focus on the sensations of whatever activity you choose. You can even do this while cleaning something, brushing your teeth, or making a snack. Also, pay attention to how these activities make you feel. Get in the habit of reminding yourself: "Is this helping me accomplish my goals?" or "Does slowing down make me feel good?" Sometimes that means you have to let go of "being right" in the moment and just accept what's effective.

Here are some other ways you can use mindfulness to help you slow down in the moment.

- Focus on the task at hand. Mindfulness strongly depends on your awareness and using your senses. The next time you're doing a mundane task, take the opportunity to practice. Even something as simple as taking a shower is an opportunity to be mindful. Pay attention to the sounds of the water as it hits the floor and your body. Notice the temperature of it, and how it feels against your skin. The next time you eat, don't do it in front of the television or while looking at your phone. Concentrate on the utensil in your hand, how it picks up the food, and the way your food looks, tastes, and smells. You're guaranteed to enjoy it a lot more, and it will put your focus on something else instead of your mood. (Studies show that mindful eating has also been linked to healthy digestion)

- Check-in with yourself. Whenever you get the chance, get in the habit of making sure you're okay. Sometimes the first step to changing your mood is to recognize that you're in one. When you check in with yourself, you'll become more aware of how your body feels when you're in an unpleasant mood. Pay close attention if you feel tired, if you have aches and pains, if you're hungry, or maybe feeling lonely and need to spend time with a friend. The next time your negative feelings arise, you'll recognize the mood more quickly and can then plan on how to deal with it.

The Three Mindsets

Mindfulness can be used to unlock a state of mind that can serve as a helpful guide to your moods and emotions. A concept explored in Dialectal Behavioral Therapy (DBT) and Cognitive Behavioral Therapy (CBT) is there are three states of mind that exist: Reasonable, Emotional, and Wise Mind. It's important to know how these states of thought work in your mind, and that they are usually trying to compete with one another. However, with patience and some practice, balance can be achieved between all three.

Let's start with the first state of mind, the reasonable mind. The reasonable mind focuses on the logical side of things. It is known for thinking through situations by using facts and logic to solve an issue, rather than using your emotions. Think of your reasonable mind as a stoic figure. It's very serious, always focused on what's practical and factual, and doesn't express emotion. When an issue arises, it's the inner voice that tells you how to solve the issue step-by-step. The reasonable mind is most useful for completing tasks where we need our logic the most. Some examples include teaching and learning concepts from others, doing important paperwork, or making plans for an important event.

The second state of mind, the emotional mind is the opposite of reasonable mind, in which it makes decisions based off of emotions rather than logic. It doesn't take time to think but is more of a "knee-jerk" response to a situation, or the first thing that comes to mind. Think of your emotional mind as what your "gut" feeling often is. It relies on instinct and applies this instinct when things happen to us. These emotions typically affect the decisions you make in the moment. The emotional mind is useful in situations when you want to feel more "spontaneous," like buying a new article of clothing because you liked it, or trying new foods. You also tap into your emotional mind in emotional moments, like when you're surprised by a gift, attending a wedding, celebrating your birthday, or a friend's party.

While there are benefits to both of these states of mind, there are also adverse effects. They exist as complete opposites, cold and hot. The reasonable mind is the cool and collected one, and emotional mind is often hot and quick to think. What also further divides them is that they just can't seem to work well together. Since the rational mind is not connected to emotion, it tends to neglect that your emotions are valid, only seeking the practical thing to do. Similarly, the emotional mind functions primarily on feeling, so it doesn't want to sit still and take the time to think things through in a logical way. It's important for one state of mind to not have more power than the other, but how can you prevent this from happening?

This is where the third state of mind, the wise mind, comes into play. Wise mind represents your internal wisdom. It is a desired state of mind to be in, mainly because the main purpose of the wise mind is to create a perfect balance between emotions and thought. By searching for what's right, it allows you to respond appropriately to certain situations. You can think of your wise mind as if it were a calming referee to your emotional and rational states of mind. It allows the two of them to actually work well together. The emotional mind is allowed to express its feelings, while the reasonable mind can respond to those emotions with rationality. Wise mind is one of the hardest states of mind to achieve because it's difficult to allow both sides of your mind to coexist in one space. But if you create this balance between emotional and reasonable mind, you'll also establish a healthy balance between what you think, what you feel, and what you know.

The Danger of the Emotional Mind

Both the reasonable mind and the emotional mind have their pros and cons that make them unique. However, in the case of managing and monitoring your moods, the emotional mind can pose a potential threat if not dealt with properly. The emotional mind exists due to our basic human instincts of wanting to survive. It's the gut instinct that tells us to cry in certain settings or to laugh at someone's joke that we liked. Unfortunately, it's also the instinct that we want to hurt others when they've hurt us. It's definitely okay to be open and express your emotions, especially when you feel hurt or excited about something. However, your moods will greatly suffer if you spend too much time thinking with your emotional mind.

The biggest danger the emotional mind possesses is that it's impulsive. When you're in an emotional state, the last thing you want to do is settle for a moment to think a situation through with logic and reason. If you're upset, you might want to throw, hit, or yell at something rather than calm yourself down and try to think of what made you upset. Therefore, the emotional mind creates unpleasant reactions that are based only on feelings and not facts. It's satisfying at the moment but can lead to highly unpleasant consequences in the long run.

For example, a kid might be angry with his sibling and break their sibling's toy. At the moment, the kid feels satisfied with getting back at their sibling. However, the long-term consequence is that the parent of that kid will punish them and provide some sort of consequence, such as grounding them or taking one of their toys away as punishment. At the moment, the kid doesn't think of the consequences, just that they want to appease their emotions, which then creates an irrational response.

When was the last time you acted impulsively? Did it have negative consequences afterward? Maybe it was saying something rude to a significant other in an argument or spent money on something when you were supposed to be saving it. What happened as a result of acting this way? The problem with putting all your focus into your emotional mind is that eventually, your emotions will control you. When that happens, you'll find yourself in more stressful situations. Without taking time to reason with yourself, your mind keeps going and going nonstop on a train of negative thinking.

You'll also have trouble believing everything you think. When that happens, you prevent yourself from growing as a person and instead get stuck in the same patterns of thought. Instead of learning how to deal with stressful situations, you fall in the opposite direction and break apart. It's certainly hard to learn anything when you're only thinking with emotions and not facts. This is why it's important to strengthen your wise mind, that when emotional issues arise, you'll be ready to apply rational thought to your emotions. In turn, this will prevent you from making impulsive, dangerous decisions.

How to Use Your Wise Mind

Now that you know what wise mind is, it's also important to know the ways you can achieve it. Mindfulness plays a huge role in developing your wise mind, which we'll explore in the following sections. It's important to strengthen your wise mind so that you can consult with it whenever you need to. It's also important to practice these methods when you are feeling in a good mood so that you can easily grasp them. When you're in a bad mood, it's hard to absorb information that will help you because you'll be more likely to push it away. The two main focuses of channeling your inner wise mind are by practicing acceptance while also facing the facts of a situation.

In DBT, to practice acceptance for your wise mind, first know that it relies on "willingness" rather than "willfulness." The main difference between these two terms is that willingness means to accept, while willfulness means to go against. Much like a current in a river or ocean, willingness entails swimming along with the water, riding it out and waiting to see where it takes you. Willfulness, on the other hand, is when you try to swim against the current and are determined to swim as hard as you can to get through it. Only one option will leave you exhausted and fruitless in the end. Can you guess which one it is?

Acceptance or "willingness" is the key to unlocking your wise mind. It's recognizing that you're part of a much bigger picture, that you're just a piece of the universe but still playing a part of it in the end. To practice this concept, understand that life often has a natural flow to it, with constant ups and downs. Sometimes, no matter how much planning we do, there's always something that can or will go wrong without us knowing it. How you react to these situations determines if you're behaving more "willing" or more "willful."

For example, say you had made plans to go to a concert or an outdoor fair. Unexpectedly, the forecast predicts it's going to rain that day, which you didn't plan for at all. Now, you could still push yourself to go to that event because you were determined to go THAT day. As a result, it means getting rained out while you're there and you'll spend your time being miserable instead of having fun. Or, you can accept that things out of your control will happen. You can instead say, "It didn't work out today, but this event is going all weekend so hopefully tomorrow will be better. For now, I'll stay home and do something fun anyway."

We always want to try to swim against the current, but in truth, it never really gets us anywhere. Instead of trying to force your way to happen regardless of consequences, look for ways that you can accept the situation and move on. Here are some methods to do just that:

- Don't try to "fix" everything. You'll only exhaust yourself and become impatient with things that aren't even in your control. It'll only leave you feeling bitter and angry.
- Learn to not give up just because something didn't work out. For instance, don't fall apart when a small part of your plan falls through. You don't cancel an entire birthday party just because the napkins weren't the color you wanted. The same goes for anything else in life.
- Be patient, even in small moments. By being stubborn, you're only focusing on what you want at that exact moment instead of being patient about it. When you're

feeling sick, you can say, "I'm still going to go out today. I want to have fun instead of lying around being sick." You'll exhaust yourself with this way of thinking. A patient way to deal with the situation is to say, "I think I'll stay home today and take my medicine for a couple of days until I feel better. I need to rest and recharge."

Another way to recognize and strengthen your wise mind is to strive to face the facts in a situation. This coincides with utilizing your reasonable mind to better understand and accept your emotions when they happen. Sometimes your emotions do all the talking for you, which clouds your judgment. But if you instead focus on the facts, you can change the way you emotionally react to things.

Our thoughts and emotions are often shaped by certain events, creating different kinds of chain reactions. One chain is that an event in our life triggers a thought, which triggers an emotion. Here's how this reaction can occur:

(The Event) You forgot your keys → *(The Thought) "Why can't I remember anything?"* → *(The Emotion) Sadness or inadequacy.*

Another chain reaction is when the last two are switched. Events can trigger emotions, which then trigger thoughts as a result. An example of this would be:

(The Event) Getting stuck in traffic → *(The Emotion) Impatience or overwhelming annoyance* → *(Thought) "Everyone around me is so stupid!"*

The trouble with emotions is that sometimes they may warp your perceptions so that you'll have difficulty finding the facts. Your emotions will try to rationalize why you're right to feel angry or annoyed in a situation. Because of this, you'll have trouble believing which facts are true.

To avoid situations like these arising, ones that can be harmful to your moods, it's important to always look for the true facts in any situation. Using your wise mind, focus on the what, who, where, why, and how to find the facts without adding your own bias to them (Facts are things that can be proven with clear and logical evidence).

To find the facts, ask yourself:

- What emotion am I experiencing?
- Who made me feel this way? (If you're having an emotional response to how someone has treated you)
- What happened that made me feel this way?
- How am I interpreting this event? (Am I making assumptions, or unhelpful thoughts about the situation?)

Let's look at these events again, but by using our wise mind to acknowledge the facts:

(The Event) You forgot your keys → (The Thought) "Oops, I was distracted for a moment with something else. That's a little frustrating, but I'll find my keys and get going again → (The Emotion) refocused or understanding

You can already tell the difference when you allow this balance between emotion and thought, rather than letting them control you negatively. Here's the second situation seen with our wise mind.

(The Event) Getting stuck in traffic → (The Emotion) Impatient or annoyed → (Thought) "I'm getting frustrated because I know I have somewhere to be and I want to be on time. But there's not much I can do until it clears up, so I'll wait.

When an event triggers you, assess the situation from a different point of view as well. Try to insert yourself into someone else's shoes rather than stewing in your own emotions. In the case of the traffic situation above, instead of getting frustrated that the road is blocked, realize that maybe it's because a serious accident has happened up ahead. Put your thoughts towards somebody else, and you'll notice a more compassionate reaction: *"I hope the people ahead of me are okay and that this traffic isn't from a car accident."* Make sure you're not making any assumptions about someone or a situation. When you try to look for the facts, your reasonable mind and emotional mind come together in "wise mind" mode, by recognizing your feelings while also making sure those feelings are just. This way you can make sure your emotions aren't always taking the wheel.

Wise Mind, Mindfulness, and Changing Your Moods

Now that you know what mindfulness is and what it can do for you, you'll see that if utilized often, mindfulness will help you recognize your moods better. By utilizing mindfulness alongside your wise mind, you can strongly grasp your emotions and change your moods. A concept of DBT entails utilizing mindfulness to "unlock" your wise mind when you need it. You can achieve a wise mind through mindfulness in three basic steps: Observing, Describing, and Participating

Observing means paying attention and noticing something using mindfulness. In this case, you'll be paying attention to the thoughts that come to your mind. Allow your thoughts to pass by as if you were watching boats along a lake or cars passing by a window. These things never stop for you to get a good look at them, and you can treat your thoughts the same way. What are your thoughts often about? Things you have to do that day? Memories or experiences? Goals for the future? Opinions on other people?

Whatever your thoughts are, try to pay attention to them without seeing how they make you feel. This can be difficult if an unpleasant thought comes to mind, but practice seeing them without the emotional response behind them. Don't try to focus on resolving your thoughts either. This entails clinging to your thoughts and trying to examine them further, which puts you on an unfocused trail of thought. Practice observing by using all of your senses: Taste, touch, see, hear, smell. While doing an everyday task, observe how your senses can apply to the situation.

Describing means putting words to what you notice while observing your thoughts. Try to imagine your thoughts in a variety of ways, as if they were packages that needed labels before being shipped off. You have to put a special sticker on each one to know what it is. To do this, label your thoughts as they come to mind and learn to sort them into different categories. Thoughts are thoughts, feelings are feelings, and actions are actions.

What also helps describe your thoughts and emotions is to phrase them as though you are experiencing them objectively, rather than just experiencing them. For instance, when you have an anxious thought, phrase it as "I'm having an anxious thought," and not focusing on what the thought actually is. Do this with your thoughts, feelings, and actions so they're labeled like this:

"It's a cold day outside" = Thought

"My body feels uncomfortable" = Feeling

"I'm falling asleep at my desk" = Action

These are only minor examples, but when you simplify your thoughts into experiences, you'll get the hang of recognizing unpleasant ones. It's important to also not let your personal opinions get in the way of your thoughts.

Practice describing by learning how to take note of your surroundings and describing what you notice. Find a person walking by, or things in nature (stones, leaves, grass, trees, etc.) What kind of things do you notice when you see these things? Avoid judgmental words like "ugly," or "weird," or other phrases that would negatively describe something.

You can also describe your feelings by breaking them down into how they make you feel when you feel them: "I feel like

_____ and my thoughts are _____" to create a cause and effect connection.

Participating means completely engaging in your experiences. Sometimes we are in the middle of an activity we enjoy, or are spending time with friends only to find ourselves distracted with our worries of work or troubles going on in our minds. Instead of distracting yourself with thoughts, only put your focus on what's going on in the present. It's important to fully participate by staying in the present so that you can truly experience the world around you. When you have stronger control over how you handle your thoughts and emotions, you can easily put them aside to enjoy your present experience.

When you do get the chance to be in the present, really strive to throw yourself into what you are doing. This means not worrying about what others think or worrying if you're feeling silly or 'stupid.' Focus on the sensations of everything in the moment. If you're dancing, really dance. If you're cooking or cleaning, really pay attention to the feelings and sensations you experience while doing it.

It's also a good idea to harness your wise mind in these moments, by using just the right amount of energy in the activity. Don't force yourself to get excited or energized about something, but also don't put the minimum effort into it. As a healthy balance, give a comfortable amount of energy. To practice participating, start by making connections with your surroundings and how they affect you. When you climb into bed, focus on how comfortable your covers feel and make the connection that they feel good and safe around you. When you're on a walk, feel your shoes against the ground, and think about how the Earth below you is always solid and holding you up.

Fighting Negativity With Opposite Reactions

With negative emotions, it can sometimes be difficult to find the good side of things. Once you've learned how to identify and recognize your negative emotions, you can use this tactic commonly used in DBT to stop them before they control your moods. It's too easy to feel a negative emotion, only to let it control the way we feel for the rest of the day. When one emotion leads to the next, you'll find yourself deep in a string of negativity.

To respond to these negative emotions, catch them as quickly as you can and do something to change them through opposite reactions. You can do this by mentally and physically dealing with them. Whatever you feel, if it's negative try to apply the opposite reaction to it. If you're upset and feeling heated, instead of leaning into those angry feelings, do a calming breathing exercise and react oppositely. This means that sometimes you'll have to step out of your comfort zone when you feel uncomfortable.

To physically deal with your negative emotions in a more positive way, change your body posture, like sitting up straight, shoulders back, holding your head high instead of looking down. Uncross your arms to be more 'open,' instead of retreating into yourself. If you're upset, unclench your fists, take some deep breaths, and neutralize your face instead of scrunching it up in anger. Even making changes like this can drastically improve your emotions by changing the sensations that correlate with these negative emotions.

Sometimes this isn't easy. You might feel stuck in a negative situation and may find it difficult to think positively or try opposite reactions. When this happens, find a quiet place (if you're in public, find somewhere like a bathroom) and gently try to calm yourself down for a few moments. Even removing yourself from the experience for a little bit can calm you down enough to get a better hold on your emotions.

Avoiding Judgment in the Present

It can be difficult to monitor your emotions, especially if you allow your personal opinions to get in the way of how you think. It makes sense that it's much harder to think positively when you're forcing yourself to think positive and get frustrated when you can't.

To combat this, you should acknowledge your thoughts and emotions without fear or worry behind them.

Judgment comes in many forms. Sometimes it is multitasking while you're doing an activity and your thoughts drift elsewhere. Sometimes it means attaching your own opinions to thoughts and emotions, trying to bring your reasoning to them. Notice when you're multitasking with thoughts. Are you holding your pet but instead of petting them, your mind is somewhere else? Try doing one thing at a time. Eat when you're eating, not watching TV or looking at your phone. Don't try to handle every thought and feeling at once. Try to avoid distractions, and when you are distracted, bring your attention to the task at hand.

Your inner voice provides insight into how you're viewing a situation. Learn to recognize situations in which you're judging your thoughts. It might sound like it's talking in a negative way, which means there are negative emotions attached to those thoughts. When this happens, remember to always focus on the facts. If you notice your friend is upset, think of "my friend is upset," as a fact. If you're thinking, "My friend is definitely mad at me for something and it's my fault," then you're applying a judgmental filter to your thoughts. Your inner voice also has a tone that you should watch out for. Take note if it sounds impatient, sarcastic, or annoyed. Remember, this is your emotional mind talking and not your reasonable mind. When judgment arises, do your best to think of things rationally.

Avoiding Negative Thinking

Like judgmental thoughts, negative thinking is another ingredient of our moods. As we've discussed earlier about our Ego, we like to think we have total control over what we think. But sometimes those complicated thoughts still like to weasel their way into our minds whether we like it or not. One kind of thought in particular, intrusive thought, can make us feel as though something is wrong with us. Intrusive thoughts are thoughts that seem to pop into our head without us actively thinking about them. They're often disturbing, sometimes about harming others and ourselves either physically or emotionally. They frighten us whenever they appear because they seem far from our normal way of thinking. We then ask ourselves, "What in the world made me think of that?"

It's better to just ignore these kinds of thoughts, but sometimes we can't help but look too far into them and want to pick them apart. Surely we wouldn't have thought that horrible thing if we didn't mean it, right? Actually, that is very far from the truth. The brain is constantly producing and processing endless catalogs of information, which means that sometimes it comes up with strange or unpleasant thoughts that we don't agree with.

We simply can't treat every thought as if it were fact. If we did, we'd be constantly bombarded with negativity that will always put us in a negative mood. We stress ourselves out over negative thinking, feeling like we have to assess every thought we have instead of letting them pass us by.

This is where mindfulness plays its part. If you increase your awareness of how you think, you'll be able to recognize the difference between what is true and what is just an intrusive thought. The next time you have a disturbing thought that bothers you, think about if you really agree with it. Remind yourself that you are the one that knows your set of moral guidelines and beliefs best. By creating a "thought filter," you can sort your thoughts into what's true and what's just a weird concept your brain came up with.

It's also important to realize that while you're on a path to happiness and feeling good about yourself, your mind still wants to retreat into that comfortable space of negative thinking. Think about it, it's much easier to lie around in bed than it is to get up and dedicate time to exercise. Your mind works the same way. It takes effort to keep your focus in a positive space, and sometimes the easiest thing to do is look at things negatively. This prevents you from really enjoying the times where you should be enjoying yourself. Have you ever been to a special event or on vacation, only to dread the moment it's going to end? After all, the end of it means that tomorrow will come and that means going back to everyday life and responsibilities. This is also your brain trying to look for some kind of way to sabotage your happiness.

Since the beginning of humanity, we have had what's known as a "fight or flight" response, in which we receive a feeling of energy or alertness when we feel we've been threatened somehow. It's our brain warning us, *"Danger! Something could hurt you!"* We then decide to "fight" the danger or run away from it. This was incredibly useful for our ancestors that lived in dangerous conditions. Now, we don't have to worry about being eaten by natural predators, and yet our fight or flight response still kicks in. We prepare for danger even when there isn't any danger at all. This kind of response is sometimes triggered when we're trying to enjoy ourselves. It's as though our mind doesn't allow us to be completely vulnerable and relaxed, as if it were saying, *"Don't get too comfortable, something bad could still happen!"* The next time you feel this anxious thinking bubbling up, take a moment to remind yourself that there's no danger around. Understand that you have to choose with this response. You can let it ruin what was supposed to be a nice relaxing time, or you can choose to let it go and choose to feel good instead.

Chapter Three

Reshaping Your Ideals

As mentioned before, to change your mood and change your way of thinking, you'll need to start from the inside out. Another way to make a change within yourself and pursue happiness is by restructuring your outlook on life and your opinion of those around you. By changing the way we think about communicating with others, we're more likely to keep ourselves out of a negative mood and shift towards a more positive one.

Have you ever heard the expression, "You can't see the forest through the trees?" If you haven't, it means that it's difficult to see the big picture of a situation while you're still struggling with it. There are lies that we believe about ourselves. We see a problem and immediately think that there is no chance we could ever overcome it, or that it's just too big for us to handle. We then form the belief that these things simply can't be helped, and that we're not good enough to deal with them.

We tend to limit ourselves to these issues, which only hinders the growth in our character. When something is too difficult, we choose to believe the lies our ego tells us and think it's better off that we just ignore the issue altogether. This is a dangerous way of thinking, as it will keep us from learning and growing, and eventually, we find ourselves getting comfortable in a negative headspace most of the time. But we don't always have to believe these lies. We can look at the whole forest, if only we learn to push through the rest of the trees first.

Another contributing factor to our moods changing is how we choose to interact with other people, as well as how we choose to perceive the information they give us. In this chapter, we're going to cover how restructuring your ideals will provide you with better interactions with others, and how that impacts your happiness. This chapter will also cover how strongly are moods are persuaded by how we decide to communicate.

Restructuring your ideals seems like a mammoth of a task, but it certainly doesn't have to be. Instead, it can be broken down into four essential "pillars" that can be used as everyday guidelines to follow. By keeping these pillars in mind, you'll develop a more positive outlook on yourself as well as the people around you.

Pillar One: Use Words to Speak Life

Social settings can leave us feeling either fulfilled or frustrated, and part of that comes from the words we choose to use. Words are powerful, capable of making someone's day or completely devastating it. Sometimes we forget how much our words affect people, especially if we use them too carelessly and without any thought. The outcome of a conversation tends to depend on how we choose to use our words. For example, the more positively we speak to others, the more positive we'll feel afterward. It's simple in theory, but maybe a bit trickier to execute during an actual conversation. However, you can use what you've learned about mindfulness to help you use your words to speak life and have more rewarding connections with others. Having acute awareness is a key strategy in this pillar of ideals.

What makes a great conversation? Usually, it's the feeling of being completely engaged in what someone else has to say. Each person provides well-thought responses to the other, exchanging information that keeps the conversation exciting. You have the feeling that you want to continue talking, learning, and exchanging experiences. Good conversations often happen between people who want to take the time to have them. Once they're done, they leave you with a positive and fulfilling feeling.

Conversely, what makes a bad conversation? Usually, it's when one person feels like they're doing most of the talking. The other person provides short and closed responses, one-word answers like "Oh. No. Sure. Yeah. Cool." Without any follow up to the conversation, it makes the more talkative person feel as though they're talking too much or what they're saying isn't interesting. It's also frustrating when one person feels like they're holding up the conversation by themselves. These kinds of conversations end quickly, leaving both people unfulfilled due to a lack of connection.

Sometimes when we talk to people we find ourselves only half-listening. Most of the time we're looking at our phones when we're having a conversation, keeping one foot in one world and the other far elsewhere. How can we apply mindfulness to this situation instead? The next time you have a conversation, do it without looking at your phone. Try to be completely engaged with the person in front of you. While they're talking, make a habit of paying attention to their words. Try to picture the story they're telling you in your head, instead of trying to think of the next point you're itching to make. The more you process what the other person is saying, they'll notice you've truly been listening and will feel highly appreciative.

Filtering your words is another way to stay mindful when speaking. Don't say the first thing that comes to your mind, or let your words kind of spill out of your mouth. When that happens, we sometimes let our emotions do the talking for us, which means we're more likely to say something we'll regret afterward. Sometimes it helps that after someone makes a statement, pause for a few seconds to think about what you're going to say. Even just a few seconds can help you get a well thought out point across.

Pillar Two: Don't Take It So Personally

Just like how our words impact others, their words are also capable of affecting us. Sometimes people say things that make us feel bad about ourselves. Maybe they make critiques of our character or point out a flaw we're uncomfortable about. The words people use towards us can really have an impact on our moods. A compliment makes us feel great about ourselves, that we did something right and someone has noticed it. On the other hand, a negative statement towards us makes us dig into our insecurities, and we start to spiral into those familiar negative moods because we think, *"They're so right, maybe I am annoying (or selfish, or stubborn, etc.)"*

Sometimes we take other people's words as insults, which means that we interpret their words as some sort of attack against us. We might grow defensive, and lash out at them with an equally harmful response about them. Of course, we want to give them a taste of their own medicine. We believe that they need to realize the same pain they caused us. In reality, this does nothing but harm the relationship with the other person.

The secret to not taking things personally is to <u>not care</u> what other people think. Here's why: <u>*Everyone is only thinking about them, not you.*</u> It may sound like a harsh statement, but it actually should make you feel relieved! We always have our attention on ourselves, and because of it, we're hyper-aware of how others might see us. This is also true when we decide to take risks outside of our comfort zone. You may have a new shirt you like, but you're worried to wear it out because you're worried about what others might think. This can be exhausting as we attempt to please everyone around us. It stems from our inner desire to be accepted and wanting to feel part of something. Since negative comments keep us from achieving that, it makes us feel upset.

But because nobody is holding up a magnifying glass to you, you can be free to express your true self. If you're worried about someone's opinion on your appearance, remember that people are thinking the same thing, but only about themselves!

It's also important to realize that if someone is making a critique or a negative statement about you, it is only a reflection of something they're going through in their own life. Everyone is living a life much different from your own, dealing with his or her own unique experiences, mistakes, and insecurities.

Someone might also make a rude comment to you because it may be related to something they're secretly insecure about. Some people feel better about themselves when they point out the flaws in others. This, of course, is rude and not a healthy or kind way to treat others. But if we shrug off their words instead of letting them harm us, we can instead find an opportunity to examine their reasoning for wanting to hurt us in the first place. When we pay attention to times like these, we tend to notice the hidden struggles people are dealing with in their world.

That being said, like everyone else you have your world, made up of the intricate thoughts and memories and experiences you've been through. To be as respectful of others as they should be to us, it's important not to force your perspective onto them. When we intend to "convert" others to our way of thinking, we become disappointed with them when they don't accept it.

Instead of forcing others to think the same way, we should instead cherish and uphold the belief that we simply cannot control people. We have no power that controls what other people say to us or about us, therefore we shouldn't waste any time trying to change that. Instead, we can draw our attention inward, toward making ourselves the best we can be. By learning to not take things personally, we're less likely to hurt ourselves with negative thinking and words won't bother us like how we usually let them. What a huge weight to take off your shoulders if you spend more time thinking of your happiness, and not the expectations of others!

Pillar Three: Don't Assume

In our modern world, a very common issue you might face is that you'll text or send a message to a person, only for them to respond to you much later or not at all. As you anxiously wait for a response, your mind cycles through a massive list of reasons why they didn't talk to you. Maybe you think they're mad at you for something you said last time you were together. You find yourself poring over every past interaction with them, racking your brain for any potentially upsetting conversations you had. You might also think they don't care about you, that they looked at your message and chose to ignore it. Maybe you bother them too much, or maybe they don't find you important enough to spend time with. Maybe they're hanging out with a friend more exciting than you.

Another example would be if you were at the store, and you saw your friend in an aisle. As you went up to them, expecting to have a conversation, they instead gave a quick greeting and hurried off. What is often your first thought in this situation? Do you automatically look toward yourself, wondering how you could have offended them? Surely you did something at that moment that made them not want to talk to you. Or maybe the bottom line is that they just don't like you. They were trying to hurry away without getting roped into a conversation with you.

STOP! This is a branch of negative thinking that involves making assumptions. If you need a reminder, assumptions are thoughts that are accepted as true without even having proof behind them. They're very similar to intrusive thoughts in that we often choose to believe them, even when they aren't true. Communication is brilliant, but it's certainly not without its flaws. It can be used for the better, to help us connect. If used incorrectly, though (or not used at all) it can push us farther apart.

Often, you might misinterpret what people are trying to tell you. Someone might make a comment to you in a joking way. Because you have your insecurities that you're self-conscious about, you might assume that they're pointing out the truth. You then believe they're trying to make you feel bad about one of your qualities.

Assumptions create a social slippery slope and are dangerous for our moods. When we misinterpret someone, it often puts us on a negative train of thought. It starts somewhere simple: Your friend made a joke about you being too serious. That thought evolves into an assumption: "My friend sincerely thinks I'm too serious." Since you believe the assumption as truth, you take it a step further in your mind and it blends with the angry mood you're in. Now you have a make-believe scenario forming in your mind: Your friend is a rude person for calling you out. You imagine yourself arguing with them to confront them about it in a rude way. Since you've been stewing on these thoughts for a while, the next time you see that friend you might treat them coldly. After all, they caused you terrible emotional pain for the past few days. You start seeing them as rude and hurtful, and it creates a small shift in your friendship overall.

All of this happens, but does your friend even know that you've been feeling this way? Not at all. Assumptions lead to anger and create make-believe scenarios in our minds that lead us to believe someone is purposely trying to harm us or that they don't like us. This puts us in a bad mood, but most of the time the other person doesn't even realize they've put us there in the first place. This prevents us from truly connecting with others because instead of communicating our thoughts and feelings as we should, we chose the easier path of believing that people are purposely out to get us. Our assumptions completely change our perceptions of people, even though there isn't any evidence to support the assumption.

How can we deal with assumptions? Like dealing with intrusive thoughts, you can apply mindfulness to something you might be assuming. The next time you're about to assume something of a person and how they feel about you, focus on the truth instead. Know that the person cares about your wellbeing and wouldn't go out of their way to harm you. When your friend is making a joke, treat it as a joke instead of an insult. By being more mindful of your thoughts, you'll know when you're making assumptions and can then change those thoughts to reflect the truth.

The next time you find yourself making assumptions, see how you can use proper communication through the situation. If your friend said something that hurt you, let them know. It's hard to speak up sometimes, but most times when we do it only helps us for the better. Someone might not realize the damage they had caused you and would understand your feelings if only you help them see it from your perspective. Rather than treating that person as wicked in your mind, you can instead remember that people are people and that they can't read your mind all of the time.

Let's take a look at those two scenarios from earlier. In the case of your friend not messaging you back, instead of getting upset about it and assuming they don't like you, follow up to see how they are doing. Something along the lines of: "Hey, did you get my message? Let me know if you want to hang out soon." You may be surprised to find the truth was far different from your assumptions (the ones you *thought* were true). Your friend might reply that they were sorry they missed your message. They might explain they were at an event for the day, they had an emergency, or that their phone or computer wasn't working. Nine times out of ten, they might have seen your message but had totally forgotten to respond to you because something came up.

As for the friend in the grocery store, take a moment to think through the situation without making it about you. Your friend might hastily explain later that they would have loved to chat, but they had a lot of errands to get done that day. They could have been rushing into the store to grab a quick thing, while their significant other was waiting in the car outside and didn't want to keep them waiting.

Like all negative thoughts, it's important to know that assumptions are in no way the truth. They have nothing to do with real life, only with what fears and doubts you have about yourself. But if you learn to communicate these thoughts with others, you'll be relieved to know that in the end, we're all just people that make mistakes, oftentimes without realizing it.

Pillar Four: Try to Do Your Best

The fourth and final pillar encompasses the other three pillars we've examined so far. It's easy to sink into a bad mood when we fail at something. We expect to do something right, only to mess up. The more we mess up, the more we start to believe that we're not good enough. But rather than focusing on obtaining our goals right away, we should instead put work into the journey that gets us to that success. We tend to treat our problems like mountains. The solution to overcoming the problem is at the very top, and almost seems impossible when you're looking at it from the base. Instead of being upset at how high you have to climb, learn to enjoy the small steps you take to reach the top.

We often hear that we should "always do our best," but sometimes we often forget what that means. Typically, we think doing our best means we have to be THE best, which is the wrong way of looking at it. The more we try to be THE best, the more intense the pressure is to maintain that incredibly high standard. Then we get upset when we can't meet that standard, and – Oh, boy here we go again.

Like your moods, one thing to remember about your "best" is that it's also a temporary state, which means that it's constantly capable of changing. We have days that are "off," where we're feeling sick or tired, and just don't have as much energy than normal. You may be going through a difficult emotional time, due to factors out of your control. It's hard to do your best during those times when our minds aren't in tip-top shape. But instead of always striving for perfection you can take some of the pressure of by simply *trying* your best.

No matter how you are feeling, even if you take a small step to try, you'll already feel a huge sense of accomplishment for that day. No need for putting yourself down if you fail, the pressure is already off because you tried and gave it your actual best. The hardest thing isn't achieving a goal it's trying to get there in the first place. It's also important to keep in mind that you're not going to achieve your best every day. There will be some days where you will still assume things of others, or forget to use your words mindfully. During those times, do not get discouraged and feel like giving up. Instead, remind yourself that you have the opportunity to try again the next day.

By keeping these four pillars in mind, you'll gain a much deeper understanding of people and yourself. Something to always remember is that we all have our ways of life. Sometimes they may conflict with how others live, but if you take a moment to try to understand them, it'll open up a whole new path to making successful connections with those at your work, home, and in your personal life.

Quick Tip: Focus your Attention Outward

Although you're focusing on creating your best life and feeling good, we often get too immersed in working on ourselves that we forget another rewarding outlet: helping others. When you spend too much time focusing on yourself, you fail to see and appreciate what others around you do to help you. When you step outside of your perspective and instead try to do at least one thing each day for someone else instead of yourself, you'll have an incredible sense of accomplishment and compassion. You don't have to contribute 100% of yourself to helping others, especially during times where you're losing copious amounts of energy to help someone else. In those times, do what you can, but allow yourself some time to rest.

Chapter Four

Get Out of Your Mind

We've seen how mindfulness can have a positive effect on our moods, and that by reshaping our ideals we're able to feel good from conversations with others. But what happens when we have a hard time being mindful? Sometimes in our busy day, we forget to even stop thinking for a moment. And even when we do have the time, we have trouble with keeping our minds focused on the present. But like anything in life, the best way to learn something is through practice and patience.

The best part about mindfulness is that you can practice it at any point in your day. But sometimes we just need to go into the day with a clear mind and great intentions. A great tool to use for monitoring and changing your moods is meditation. Meditation is commonly associated with Buddhist monks and spiritual gurus, when in actuality anyone can practice it, including you! In this chapter, we'll discuss the benefits of meditation, how it keeps your moods in check, and how to get started in making it a part of your mindfulness routine.

Why Meditate?

If you're seeking out a more mindful life, then meditation will surely be something worth making time for in your daily routine. There are many misconceptions about meditation. We've mentioned how we tend to think of a monk deep in concentration, feeling at one with the universe. We also tend to think meditation means completely wiping your mind clean, not having any thoughts of any kind. This is also not true. You are constantly thinking, and while it would be nice to completely stop once in a while, we'll always have that Brain TV mumbling in the background whether we like it or not.

You may notice that throughout your day, you experience a wide range of emotions. But most of the time, we don't realize we're feeling them until they've impacted our mood. Rather than recognizing right away that something has upset us, we tend to latch onto that emotion and ride it out until it puts us in a bad mood. We sink deeper into that mood, to a point where we've forgotten what made us upset in the first place.

Meditation is just the act of reorganizing your mental state, as well as passively observing your emotions so that you better know how to recognize them during your day. The benefits of meditation are endless, and you'll notice they're quite similar to the benefits of mindfulness:

It's quality control for your mind – with so many thoughts going through your mind it helps to have a strong filter to let the good ones stick around the bad ones to pass you by. Whenever you feel bad, annoyed, or frustrated, you'll be able to recognize these feelings better, as well as identify any "triggers" or elements that give you those emotions. The sooner you can pinpoint what emotion you're feeling, the quicker you can appreciate the good ones and shake off the bad ones.

It brings a sense of inner peace –You may be so used to your usual routine that it might be difficult to see how your mind is catching up to the rest of your body. Sometimes you just need to truly stop for a moment and check in with your mental state. The world is a stressful place sometimes, and we get caught up in the twists and turns without realizing how much it affects us. By establishing a sense of self, your "inner self" you can draw your attention back to your goals and what personally matters to you.

It's good for your body – It's not always just about your mind. Scientifically, practicing meditation has plenty of physical benefits as well. Those who meditate tend to have better concentration and creativity. Your brain can grow sharper, enhancing your judgment and strengthening your decision-making abilities. Because you're handling your stress better through meditation, it can lower your blood pressure and increase circulation in your body. Spending a moment in meditation can also leave you feeling relaxed and more rested afterward.

An Easy Guide to Meditation

You don't have to practice Buddhism or be spiritual to use meditation. On the other hand, if you are spiritual, you can incorporate meditation into your daily prayer. The great thing about meditation is its versatility, that you can tailor it to your needs, or however makes you the most comfortable. You can also start at any time and don't need any special tools, just yourself and a quiet place. There are plenty of traditional and more formal methods to meditate, but this basic template is a great and simple way to start if you're unfamiliar with it.

- Find a quiet place: the most recommended place to meditate is somewhere quiet and comfortable. Keep this space free of distractions or loud noises. You don't need absolute silence, but it helps to not have too many sounds to take you out of the exercise. Minor sounds like air conditioners or traffic noises in the background might be a little more out of your control, but you can utilize these sounds for your benefit during your meditation.

- Get comfortable: Sit on the floor, a chair, or a cushion; whichever is most comfortable for you. If sitting on the floor, you can cross your legs in front of you, placing your hands in your lap or relaxed at your sides. If seated in a chair, keep your feet flat on the floor and your palms on the top of your legs. If you're more comfortable lying down, feel free to do that as well by lying flat on your back with your face up toward the ceiling. Just be mindful of how your body feels however you choose to lie or sit, focusing on how the floor, chair, couch, or bed feels beneath you.

- <u>Set a timer:</u> You can do this with a phone or a stopwatch. Most meditation pros can practice up to an hour or more during a session. If you're just starting, it's wise to start with 5 minutes, then work your way up to 10, then 15, then 20 minutes as you start to get the hang of it.

- <u>Breathe:</u> Now it's time to meditate. Close your eyes, and allow yourself to breathe naturally. You don't have to follow a specific pattern. As you breathe, really be mindful of how the air is flowing through your body, and follow this path as it travels in and out. Keep in touch with the sensations you might feel from breathing, as the air moves through your nose, maybe touching the back of your throat, into your lungs, then back out through the nose as you exhale. With each breath you take, notice how your chest feels as it rises and falls. The key to successful meditation is to always concentrate on your breath. Let it be the tool for keeping you grounded.

- <u>Monitor Yourself:</u> The mind is always going to wander during this time. But the beauty of meditation is that you're not trying to completely clear your thoughts, only let them pass by one at a time. As you breathe, allow your mind to wander, but don't follow it too much. Try to see your thoughts without judgment. Instead of getting frustrated that you're thinking about something, let the thought pass by, along with the next one and the next. Treat each one with a kind demeanor, accepting it before letting it go. The moment you start to feel yourself trailing off in a train of thought, simply redirect your focus back to your breath and how it feels. If there are any sounds in the room out of your control, like an air conditioner, heater, or noises coming from outside your home, try to incorporate them as part of the atmosphere. Let those kinds of distractions blend in, and they soon won't bother you as much.

- <u>Gently Bring Yourself Back:</u> Continue this process, maintaining your focus on your breathing until the timer finally stops. Once it goes off, don't get up right away. Instead, cherish the moment for a little longer. Take a second to appreciate and be thankful you put in the work to improve yourself. Then, slowly open your eyes and take one last deep breath. Move slowly and with purpose as you bring yourself back.

- <u>Set an Intention:</u> An optional way to end your meditation is to set an intention, which is a goal you'd like to achieve for yourself. Your mind feels the freshest after meditating, and it's a great time to focus on something else you'd like to work on. Before carrying on with your day, try to pick something that needs some attention in your life. It doesn't have to be a huge multi-step goal, just something simple to apply to your day. Quietly tell yourself what your intention is, that you can remind yourself of throughout the day:
  - "Today I want to try being more positive."
  - "I want to think more kindly of others at work or school."
  - "I want to put myself out there a little more and step out of my comfort zone."
  - "I want to stay focused and patiently deal with distractions."

Try this method of meditation at least twice a day. When you want to meditate is completely up to you, but it's highly recommended to start your day with meditation and to practice it before you go to sleep. It can be a great tool to wake up as well as to wind down. If you're someone that needs a pick-me-up in the middle of the day, absolutely feel free to meditate then.

A lot of times you might feel discouraged while meditating, where you'll feel like you're not "getting it" right away. But it's important to remember that it requires a little bit of practice to get better. After each time you meditate, you can track your progress by writing how you felt before and after you practiced. By meditating a little bit each day, you help strengthen your ability to be mindful, which will already jumpstart your day with a good mood!

Chapter Five

The Power of Health

When you're in a negative mood, you're less likely to make healthy choices. That's because whenever you're feeling down, the last thing you want to do is eat fruits and vegetables or go for a walk. An extra-large pizza in bed sounds like the best option to cure a bad mood when in reality it could be making you feel much worse.

Think of your body as if it were a house. What does your house look like? Has it been tidy for a while, or is there clutter in every room? How about the outside? Are the shutters falling off, or is the roof caving in? Does it still have a fresh coat of paint? When your house hasn't been kept up with or examined for issues, it's easier for it to fall apart and break down. When that happens, the house feels less like a home and more of a negative space. It's best to assess the damage and maybe focus on doing a little bit of maintenance to get it up and running smoothly again.

Lifestyle choices are one of the common factors that impact your moods. It's one thing to focus inward to change your moods, but sometimes you might forget that you also have to put some work into the rest of your body, the rest of the 'house,' as well. You may be used to a specific routine, and if you're working often you may not want to spend your free time being active. Unfortunately, if you don't take the time and get out and move for a while, you may be more at risk of experiencing negative moods.

Since our environment is a huge factor in what moods we feel, it's important to establish a healthy lifestyle. Once you're in a negative mood, it may be hard to feel like you can't get out of bed or off the couch. But by putting in just a little work into an active routine each day (even for ten minutes) it'll become so much easier to get active and stave off bad moods.

Now that you've understood how to make an internal change through mental awareness, the next best thing you can to feel your best is to treat your body kindly. You can achieve this by eating well and setting aside some time for physical activity. In this chapter, you'll discover how factors such as exercise and diet affect your moods, and how you can utilize a healthy lifestyle to change your mood for the better!

The Science of Exercise and Mood

A lot of questions come to mind when we think of exercise. How much do we need each day? How often do we need to be active? What counts as exercise? All of these questions will be answered, but we first need to examine how exercise affects our bodies, which in turn affects our minds and our moods.

To put it into simple perspective, the more active you are the better you will feel. When in a negative mood, it's easy to drift towards wanting to lie around. Watching TV, playing video games, and scrolling through your phone are all highly appealing because they don't require much effort on your part. If you're very busy during your workweek, the last thing you want to do is go outside for a run. We feel tired and drained, and these other activities are very easy to do, especially for long periods. Before you know it, you've been on your phone or in front of the TV for hours. How does this typically make you feel? While it seems relaxing in the moment, often when we walk away from the screen we feel even more drowsy or "down" than we were before. You may notice you have a headache afterward. Your body may be weak, and ready to go to bed even when it's the middle of the day. Even though it's easy to participate in these activities, if carried out for long periods, they can put you at higher risk for developing anxiety and depression.

Now think of the opposite. If you do have a chance to be active, how do you tend to feel afterward? Most of the time it's a positive feeling and despite having to use energy to exercise you might feel more awake and motivated for the rest of the day once you're done.

Let's go even deeper, and look at this from a scientific standpoint. Your body is composed of chemical reactions that are constantly taking place inside of you. These reactions determine how you think and feel and when you feel them. When you exercise, you're creating a chemical reaction in your body that enhances your mood through natural chemicals called endorphins. These chemicals are formed in your brain and spinal cord, functioning as neurotransmitters, which are "messengers" for your nerves. They activate certain receptors in your body, ones that contribute to how you feel pain or emotions.

One of the main functions of endorphins is that when released, they produce a calming and euphoric effect, similar to the effect of morphine (without addictive properties). It's sort of the body's natural response to release endorphins when we're feeling stressed or in pain to help calm us down. However, we can trigger the release of endorphins whenever we exercise or even just by eating certain foods like chocolate or spicy peppers.

Benefits of Exercise

There's a reason why endorphins are "feel-good chemicals." For those that struggle with anxiety or depression, doctors often recommend exercise as part of treatment because of the pleasant effect endorphins give off. Aside from chemical reactions in your brain, exercising regularly can provide you with plenty of other benefits to your body.

One of the best ways exercise affects your mental health is that it helps you concentrate on something else rather than stress, anxiety, and other feelings associated with negative moods. While exercising, you're distracting yourself by paying attention to how your body feels. You're noticing your breath, how your muscles feel, and are focusing intently on a goal, rather than intrusive thoughts or negative emotions. You may have to count a certain number of pushups or crunches or repeat certain motions during a workout. This helps put your focus on the present and steers your mind away from negative thinking. When you're finished exercising, you may feel a sense of accomplishment. No matter how difficult it seems to get moving, once you're finished you feel excited and motivated to want to exercise more. The more goals you set to exercise, the more inclined you are to want to reach those goals. It creates a sense of something to look forward to, even while you are exercising.

Believe it or not, exercise can also affect your sleeping patterns. The National Sleep Foundation explains how it's important to exercise if you're trying to get into a healthy pattern of sleep: "Regular exercise, particularly in the morning or afternoon, can impact your sleep quality by raising your natural body temperature a few degrees. Later in the day, when your internal thermostat drops back to its normal range, this can trigger feelings of drowsiness and help you drop off to sleep. Also, if you exercise outdoors, you'll be exposed to natural light, an important element in helping your body establish a good sleep-wake cycle."

Exercise also impacts how your brain works by reframing how your brain functions. Remember the "flight or fight" response that was discussed in chapter one? If you're exposed to something that frightens you or makes you nervous, you may experience physical sensations that correlate with those emotions. Your heart rate may increase. Maybe your palms start to sweat. This is your body's natural response to assess any dangers around you, and most of the time they subside after a few moments. However, if you have

PTSD, chronic anxiety, or are more prone to feeling anxious, you may experience these symptoms longer than you're comfortable with. These feelings might follow you throughout the rest of your day, creating an anxious mood, which can also make you irritable or uneasy.

Through exercise, your mind has the potential to "reprogram" itself. When you're working out, you're also working up a sweat and keeping your heart rate up, things commonly felt during an anxious time. Some research examines that over time, your brain begins to associate these feelings with exercise (something good) instead of symptoms of anxiety (something bad). As a result, whenever anxious feelings emerge you feel more at ease, as your mind becomes more aware that these symptoms relate to something good instead of something bad.

Exercise can also reduce your overall stress not just from endorphins, but also by being a physical outlet to exert excess energy. When you're overwhelmed, either with work, school, or just anything in life, you might feel uncomfortable or unable to focus. Stress can be a sign that you're overworked, and it's hard to do quality work when you're not feeling your best. When you exercise, you're providing a way to burn off some of your stress and brush aside some of that stressful thinking. Because of the mentally stimulating benefits exercise provides, such as better concentration, memory, and focus, you're more likely to feel less stressed. You also feel like you're more in control of your mental health.

Outside of the mind, exercise has a plethora of physical health benefits for your body. If you exercise regularly, you're more likely to have lower blood pressure. Depending on what kind of exercise you do, it can build and tone your muscles, as well as combat and reduce body fat. It can strongly impact your heart health, making your heart stronger as well as supporting better circulation. One of the biggest health benefits of exercise is that it can ward off dangerous diseases such as cancer and diabetes, as well as heart disease and dementia. The more you exercise and reap these physical benefits the more likely you'll feel good about yourself overall.

How and When to Stay Active

So now that we know how exercise is beneficial, it's time to examine our other questions: How much exercise do we need? How often should we exercise? What counts as exercising?

Exercising is simply any kind of activity that requires physical effort that sustains your health and wellness. It can be anything to you as long as you're staying active. You also don't have to have an incredibly intense workout for it to count as exercise. Even something as simple as walking for a little bit can impact your overall wellness.

As for how long and how often you should exercise, studies show that even ten minutes of exercise can greatly improve your mood. However, the standard recommendation for being active is 30 minutes each day. You don't have to always spend 30 minutes exercising. According to some studies, it is just as effective to break up 30 minutes of activity into smaller intervals throughout the day. For instance, if you can't take the time to run for a half an hour it's okay to walk or jog in three, ten-minute intervals.

During the week, if you are just starting to get into an exercise routine, it's recommended to spend three to four days a week exercising. Even though it's okay to work out every day, it's also important to factor in time in between those days to rest depending on what kind of workout you're interested in. What kind of exercise you want to do depends on your personal goals, such as if you want to lose weight or tone muscle. If you mainly want to exercise to help with your moods, focus on staying active each day for 30 minutes. You might also get bored if you do the same routine during the week. Try to find some creative ways to stay active so that you don't find yourself getting bored with getting exercise.

Here are just a few out of hundreds of ways to get up off the couch and get going:

- Biking
- Jogging
- Running
- Tennis or Racketball
- Yoga or Tai Chi
- Hiking
- Swimming

You also don't have to make a special trip to the gym either to stay active. It may be surprising, but you can get in your daily dose of activity just from everyday factors like cleaning your house, taking a walk in the park or around your neighborhood, or even mowing your lawn. You can even get more activity by swapping out daily habits for better ones. Instead of taking the elevator at work, try taking the stairs instead. If you can, try walking or biking to a store instead of taking your car. Even making sure you stand up enough during the day can help your health immensely. The more sedentary you are, the more likely you'll feel uncomfortable and in an unpleasant mood.

You Are What You Eat

When paired with exercise, eating healthy foods can make an incredibly positive impact on your mental health and your moods. We're all familiar with the phrase, "You are what you eat." Of course, that shouldn't be taken literally, but it carries a good message to keep in mind the next time you want to reach for a candy bar instead of a piece of fruit. Fruit is considered a healthy food, or a "whole food," one that doesn't have any added chemicals or substances to alter it. They're fresh, and also refreshing to eat. You might feel good after eating healthy foods as if you're truly nourishing your body.

On the other hand, think of a pizza. It's delicious and cheesy. We like to think we feel good by eating it because it certainly might make us happy. Emotionally, it might satisfy something in us. But in reality, it's a food that's greasy and loaded with carbohydrates. Even if there's a sprinkling of vegetables on top that might seem good, underneath is still fatty cheese and meats packed with preservatives, all on a platform of bread. In the long run, it's not sustainable for our health.

This is the main difference between whole foods and junk foods. Healthy foods are loaded with essential nutrients that your body depends upon. Junk food that's full of preservatives and added chemicals can leave your body unfulfilled. Simply put, you can eat an entire bowl of fruit and feel great, but you can't eat an entire pizza and expect to feel incredible afterward.

And the kind of food you put in your body can have a huge effect on your moods. Eating a diet that focuses on whole foods, and free of added sugars and preservatives will make your body feel good and help you manage your moods better. It's incredibly hard for us to do this, though, especially when we're going through a negative mood. We tend to sway our interest away from healthy foods and instead look towards "comfort foods."

Macaroni and cheese, pizza, fried chicken, French fries, it's all so delicious to us in the moment. While all this food is tasty, these kinds of foods make us feel bummed out. And yet we turn to them because they make us feel comfortable. The reason for this is because they're made up of carbs. Now, there are good carbs and bad ones, which are also known as refined carbs. These are often made up of processed sugars, things like high fructose corn syrup or sucrose. They're also made up of refined grains, which means that most of the nutrients have been stripped away from the wheat that was originally filled with things that are good for us. Things like B vitamins, Vitamin E, healthy fats, and antioxidants are all lost when the grain is refined. These refined carbs are often found in foods that contain white flour, such as pasta, rice, and bread. They also sneak into foods like sodas and snack foods.

The unfortunate thing about eating these kinds of carbs is that they're "empty," meaning that they don't contain much nutritional value. However, we tend to drift towards these kinds of foods whenever we're in a bad mood because we get a quick comforting fix from the sugars they contain. Even though they give us a quick pick-me-up, later in the day we might find ourselves crashing, our energy suddenly depleted. This is because these types of carbs are processed quickly in our bodies, and spike our blood sugar levels. When those levels drop, we might feel lethargic afterward.

Foods that are filled with added chemicals and preservatives can also be responsible for how our moods are affected. Our food contains tons of excess sugars, altered flavorings, and chemicals to keep our food "fresh" and tasting good. Junk food is fun to eat and tastes very good. But when we have a diet that primarily focuses on these kinds of foods, they can only make us more tired, and more prone to feeling depressed or anxious.

The main reason why processed foods are so bad for us is that they don't provide our body with what it needs to properly function. When we overload ourselves with foods loaded with extra fats, sugars, and oils, we're more likely to make our bodies feel awful afterward.

Too much sugar can lead to severe health issues down the line. It triggers anxiety and makes anxious feelings much worse. It's commonly linked to health issues like cancer, heart disease, and diabetes. It also has addictive properties, in which your body quickly starts to rely on it to function. This is where eating these kinds of foods can get dangerous, especially when your body craves them over healthier options. There's a feedback loop that's made whenever you reach for unhealthy options and eating them when you're in a bad mood. These foods pick us up for a little bit but then put us in an even worse mood, and then we find ourselves restarting the cycle all over again.

Going with Your Gut

The body tends to work in mysterious ways, and some parts of it can impact others without you realizing it. Your stomach is filled with microbes; tiny organisms that help control your digestive system and break down foods. According to recent health studies, these microbes can also affect your mental health. You have what's called your vagus nerve, which connects the brain to the stomach through neurological pathways. It's basically how your brain communicates to your stomach to help regulate your digestive tract.

How does this have to do with your moods? Well, if your gut biome isn't particularly healthy with good working microbes, it disrupts the balance between your brain and your gut, which could put you at risk for feeling negative moods and symptoms of depression. Overeating processed foods harm these microbes, as well as taking certain medications. When your gut isn't balanced in a healthy way, it can lead to issues such as inflammation and cognitive and mood problems. Doctor's typically suggest that to improve your moods, you can start with your diet. By focusing on eating whole foods, you're creating a healthy balance in your body, which can lead to a healthy balance with your mental health.

Making Positive Changes

It's okay to treat yourself to junk food now and then. But if we're trying to achieve better moods and focus on our mental health, it's important to factor in eating healthy as much as we can. This can be difficult to do, especially if your diet doesn't include enough healthy options. Here are some ways that you can get a head start on eating healthier.

- Food swaps: You can switch out unhealthy options for healthier ones. Instead of putting mayonnaise on a sandwich, try replacing it with avocado. Eat whole-wheat pasta or brown rice instead of white rice and pasta. Get creative!

- <u>Read the label</u>: If you look at some of the labels on your food, you'll be surprised to find that there are dozens of ingredients you may not recognize. Look at a jar of peanut butter. A popular brand might have a huge list of ingredients of sulfates and sugars, while another peanut butter simply contains blended peanuts. A lot of these foods contain added chemicals and flavorings to increase their shelf life or improve the way they taste. A safe bet when shopping for certain foods is to check the label for any added chemicals. The simpler the label is, the better.

- <u>Eating whole foods</u>: This is one of the most influential changes you can make to your diet and your mood. Whole foods are ones that haven't been tampered with and don't contain added chemicals or preservatives. Fruits, vegetables, whole-grain bread and pasta, and fresh meats are all good foods to incorporate into your diet.

- <u>Balancing your gut bacteria</u>: fermented foods have proven to increase the health of your gut bacteria, and to help establish a healthy environment for it to thrive. Some of these contain probiotics, which have been linked to decreasing symptoms of depression. Add foods like kimchi, kombucha, pickles, sauerkraut, Greek yogurt, and kefir to your diet to help your stomach run smoothly.

- <u>Cutting out foods</u>: You may find that certain foods might make you feel worse. Some people notice they feel in a bad mood after eating foods that are high in sugar. Dairy and wheat are common irritants, and if you suspect these might put you in a bad mood then try cutting them out for a couple of weeks and slowly reintroduce them back into your diet to see how they make you feel.

It helps to slowly introduce these habits into your diet, as well as monitor how these foods make you feel. You can keep track of what you eat by keeping a food journal, writing down the foods you ate today and how your body felt after you ate them. Did you feel more energized or tired afterward? How did these foods impact your mood for the day?

Chapter Six

Love Yourself

So far, we've covered how to understand your moods, how to change your moods through mindfulness and meditation, and how to form healthy habits to maintain good moods through exercise and healthy eating. But what should you know during the times where it seems impossible to get out of a negative mood? What about the incredibly challenging days, ones where we feel like none of these methods will work for us? Even though we might have all the tools at our disposal, we sometimes might find ourselves in a particularly difficult place. In those times, we have trouble utilizing the important tools to help us get out of a difficult mood.

Whenever you find yourself in times like these, always remember that there is still one simple belief you can hold onto. There's just one essential thread left, one that ties up everything you've learned about moods from this book, and that is to **always love yourself**.

In this chapter, we'll be discussing what you can do when you're dealing with a difficult mood you can't quite seem to shake off. You'll learn how to practice self-love to help you find comfort during difficult times. You'll also discover how to practice self-care to help yourself recharge in between the busy moments in your life.

What is Self-Compassion?

Compassion is the feeling you have when you want to help others. It's a selfless feeling where you're willing to put your own emotions aside. You feel compelled to listen to someone else's troubles instead of your own, and take the time to help them work through it any way you can. Just like you have the power to care for others, you also have the power to care for yourself.

Self-compassion is an extension of those feelings, in which you harness that sympathy towards yourself. It might sound like a selfish practice, but if you look closely, you'll see that it's essential to developing a healthy relationship with your mind and your moods. Having self-compassion means that you are more patient with yourself, and have an understanding that sometimes it's okay to make mistakes. It's kindly reminding yourself that you're not entirely perfect (and that's okay too).

The truth is, we all fail. We all make mistakes. We all fall short of our goals from time to time…because even though we strive for perfection, we're more likely to be anything but perfect. Whenever failures happen in our lives, we tend to take it as a personal issue with ourselves. However, it's important that we utilize compassion for ourselves when times like these come about.

In her book, "Self Compassion," Dr. Kristen Neff, Ph.D., addresses the concept of having compassion for yourself: "Instead of just ignoring your pain with a 'stiff upper lip' mentality, you stop to tell yourself, 'This is really difficult right now. How can I comfort myself in this moment?'"

We tend to have a lot of pride in ourselves, in which sometimes we believe we can do everything on our own without help. Sometimes we don't want to admit that we're suffering through a negative mood. We fear it'll make us look like we don't have ourselves under control, and that makes us scared or embarrassed. However, it's important that we take the time to check in with ourselves and even not be afraid to ask for help when we need it. Neff also illustrates that self-compassion is made up of three elements, which are self-kindness, common humanity, and mindfulness. Let's take a look at what each of these means:

Self-Kindness is exactly what it sounds like. It's the practice of being kind to yourself in all situations. Instead of getting mad at yourself when you do not understand something, you can calmly tell yourself that you're still learning and soon you'll get the hang of it. Self-kindness means talking to yourself as if you were kindly talking to somebody else and helping them with their issues. You can gently tell yourself that you are good enough and that you have the potential to grow and succeed. Sometimes it means having to tell yourself these things even when you're not feeling your best.

Common humanity is the understanding of the people around you. It's important to realize that when you are going through something difficult, there are hundreds, if not thousands, of other people all around the world going through the same thing. It's easy to think, *"My problem is far too specific. Nobody in the world has ever gone through something like this."* This can be a dangerously negative way of thinking. It's similar to self-pity, which is the opposite of self-compassion. Self-pity relies on victimizing oneself and can be more harmful than helpful. In reality, everyone in the world feels fear, suffering, pain, doubts, and inadequacies at some point in their lives. When you think about your troubles in this way, you feel more connected to the world. After all, we are all humans, and although these feelings are unpleasant, they're all part of the human experience.

The third element of self-compassion is mindfulness. Now, we probably know a lot about mindfulness from reading other sections of this book. But how can we use it to be more self-compassionate? The greatest thing about mindfulness is that there isn't just one special way to practice it. It's simply just being more aware of your thoughts and feelings. In relevance to self-compassion, it's important to utilize the non-judgmental side of mindfulness. Instead of believing every thought you have is the truth (including the negative ones) simply look at the thoughts and let them pass.

When you remove the emotion behind a thought, it's less likely to affect you. This can be difficult sometimes because our mind will pull up a particularly unpleasant thought. It may be about how you're not good enough, or about a mistake you've made in the past. We don't like thinking these things, but most of the time we can't help it. However, when we take away the emotion of these thoughts and stop concentrating on how they make us feel, they don't carry much power in our minds anymore.

How Does This Affect My Mood?

Moods are highly affected by your mental state, and that includes the way you talk to yourself and how you treat your thoughts. When you're in a bad mood, it becomes easier to drift to those negative opinions of yourself. On the flip side, having a positive attitude about yourself can help you combat those negative feelings when they appear.

Patience is essential when practicing self-compassion, and especially with understanding and trying to change your moods. It's important to know the way you view yourself can have a huge impact on your moods as well. Remember what we said about the ego? If we're constantly viewing ourselves in a negative light, then it's much easier to believe that we're not good enough, or can't do anything right. By practicing self-compassion, you're realizing your wellbeing and happiness and how they are connected to your moods.

Do these kinds of thoughts emerge when you feel frustrated with yourself?

"I'm so stupid for messing up."

"I shouldn't have said that. It was a dumb thing to say."

"I wish I wasn't such a failure."

"I wish I could just get my life together. How am I such a loser?"

"Why can't I get this right? I've tried hundreds of times and I don't get it."

When you have thoughts like these, it's a sign that you are being impatient with yourself. If you sway more towards negative thoughts like these, you're more likely to establish an unhealthy image of yourself. To put it into a closer perspective, just imagine what it would be like if you had said these things to a close friend or a family member. Surely it would put somebody down in an instant. After all, these words could really hurt someone. Now it's much more upsetting to think that we apply these exact phrases to ourselves. They have an extremely negative effect on us, and by giving into them they only cause us to sink further into a negative mood. What's worse, the more often you think this way, the more prone you are to experience negative moods.

Now, let's try looking at these same phrases, but with self-compassion applied to them instead:

"I made a mistake, but I can always try again."

"Next time, I'll use my words better."

"I can always keep trying."

"I'm not quite in the place I want to be. What can I do to get there?"

"It might take me longer to get this, but I'm still learning."

This is what it sounds like when you have patience with yourself. Notice how these phrases acknowledge an issue, but without judgment and in a more comforting manner. It can be hard to think this way when we're frustrated. But if you stop and take a second to put aside the emotional aspect of your thoughts, you'll feel much better about them.

You can instead rephrase these thoughts to sound more kind and create a healthier opinion of yourself rather than focusing on putting yourself down. The more patience you have, the more prone you'll be to accept moods as they come, and admit that you're improving them. We all have that voice in our mind that criticizes us, but we can tell ourselves in a much more gentle way how we can improve when we're at our worst.

The Danger of Self-Pity

With self-compassion comes its destructive opposite of self-pity. Self-pity wears a mask. It makes it seem like we're comforting ourselves when really we're seeking out dangerous emotions and stunting our emotional growth. Self-pity is when you feel sorry for yourself while constantly believing that you're somehow a victim in any and every situation. You may think that everyone is trying to make a personal attack on you, even when they're only trying to help. Everything in your life feels like it has some negative connotation to it, and that there's no way you can get over it.

Negative thinking and self-pity go hand in hand. Do you know that classic "glass half-empty or glass half-full," analogy? Self-pity is always taking note that your glass is "half-empty." You may find yourself lamenting over the bad in things instead of focusing on the good. Instead of enjoying hobbies or events, you're worried that the fun will be over soon. For example, instead of relishing a day off, you focus on having to go back to work the next day. Maybe you just got a new puppy or other pet in your home. With self-pity, you don't think about how much joy the new pet brings. Instead, you focus on the HUGE responsibility you've just brought on yourself. Now it's just one more thing in your life to worry about, right?

When you focus this lens on every aspect of your life, it can be impossible to find happiness in anything. You're constantly seeking for things that have gone wrong, and that can severely impact your moods. You also treat everything in your life with high importance. This goes back to what we've discussed about the four pillars, one of them being not to take things so seriously. Rather than shrugging off a small issue, you treat it as though it's the end of the world. And when everything leads to the "end of the world," it can be ridiculously difficult to stay positive.

One threat self-pity has to your mental health is that it keeps you from reaching the best version of yourself. When you fall into self-pity, you treat everything like an obstacle. But instead of rising to the occasion and conquering it, you crumple to the ground and feel bad that you can't (but won't) do it. Obstacles exist in our lives for us to overcome, but if you're too busy feeling sorry for yourself you'll fail to see the opportunity ahead of you to grow and change for the better.

The most dangerous effect self-pity has on your moods is that it strongly relies on keeping you in a negative mood. Self-pity *thrives* in negative moods, and one of the reasons why is because it's so easy to feed them. You can do the hard thing of overcoming an issue, or you choose the easier option of wallowing in self-pity. Wallowing means wanting to sink into negative moods and staying there for long periods. You may find yourself moping around your house, laying around and feeling melancholic. You could maybe go outside and get some air, or do something special to put you in a better mood. But when you're brooding with self-pity, you tend to instead think, *"What's the point? Nothing's ever going to make me feel better."*

Another threat self-pity carries is that it makes you crave comfort from others, and it becomes an addictive habit. We keep holding onto self-pity because it means that people around us will show that they care. This is also an easy way out of things. Someone notices we're sad, and then spends time comforting us to help us get out of that mood. But all of those pep talks mean nothing if you're not actually going to apply the wisdom to your life. The longer you hold onto self-pity, the more isolating it becomes as you start to believe that nobody understands what you're going through.

We all feel self-pity, and that's okay. What's not okay is when we let it sink into our lives and prevent us from becoming the best we can be. It's even worse when we let ourselves thrive in the negative moods that self-pity brings. We grow comfortable having it reside in us, rather than letting life shape us into unique individuals.

Self-Compassion Through Self-Care

You can show self-compassion to yourself in a variety of ways. One of these methods is through self-care, which is participating in an activity that strengthens your overall wellness. It's the concept of taking care of your mind and your body to improve your mood.

Even though you might be putting in the work to better yourself, it can also take a lot of time and effort to get to a good place. You don't always function perfectly 100% of the time, and when you feel yourself running out of steam sometimes it's best to take a small break for yourself. Practicing self-care is essential for improving your moods, and keeping them positive. Even small efforts to care yourself can brighten up your busy day, like listening to positive music on your way to work, or eating lunch outside instead of at your desk.

Self-care can be practiced in many forms, and it's up to you to see what you truly enjoy when you feel like you need a pick-me-up. It can be a small act of joy to yourself, or even setting aside a good bit of time to recharge.

Here are some suggestions for how you can practice self-care:

- Read a book
- Listen to your favorite music
- Treat yourself to your favorite meal or snack
- Relax with a pet
- Go for a walk
- Clean a room in your house
- Watch a movie or your favorite show
- Grab a coffee or tea from somewhere you like

Self-care can also literally mean taking care of your body. When was the last time you washed your face or flossed your teeth? How about a good night's sleep? Did you eat a healthy meal at some point today? When you focus on taking care of your body, your mind will also feel at ease, and you'll feel much better about yourself. It's hard to feel good about our bodies if we don't treat them with respect, which can also affect our mental health in the long run.

It's important to remember that you can't force self-care onto yourself. It's supposed to be something that makes you feel good, not something that takes energy from you or negatively affects you. Come up with your own list of ways you can feel comfortable and put your mind at ease for a moment. Include parts of your routine that focus on taking care of your body as well, such as getting enough sleep or eating healthy. It also helps to focus on small habits, such as turning your phone off an hour before you go to bed or taking a quick moment out of your day to relax.

When You're Feeling Extra Low

Like everything else in the world, changing your moods requires a combination of attention and practice. Naturally, you may grow tired or frustrated whenever you can't quite seem to shake off a bad mood. We build up these habits of wanting to seek out what's comfortable. It's easy to stay in a bad mood because it requires some work on our part to change it, work that we don't want to take the time to do. The truth is, a bad mood will stay around as long as you allow it. The same goes for positive moods, even though they seem a little more difficult to maintain at times.

It's normal to feel the weight of your moods, but what should we do in those times where we feel especially discouraged? What about those complicated bad moods that we can't seem to get rid of no matter how hard we try? When you're caught in a particularly bad mood, it can take a lot of energy to get you back on track. You may start to lose hope, and maybe even start to accept that you'll feel this way for the rest of your life.

STOP! It doesn't have to be this way! Just like pillar four suggests, always try to do your best. This means that during these particularly low times, don't give in to the easy option of living a life of negativity. Each day, try to do your best, even if it means taking a small step in a positive direction. Those small steps to changing your mood can really add up, so long as you have the determination to do it!

Changing your moods is a lot like learning to ride a bicycle or playing the piano. To be good at it means putting in the practice to learn and grow. Sometimes that means you have to mess up or fall a couple of times before you get the hang of it. In times that you feel extra-low, take a moment to really think about why you want to make a change in yourself.

Sometimes we lose focus on our goals. The goal here is to change your moods and feel good about yourself. During your journey, you may have trouble grasping certain concepts. Maybe it's difficult to stay mindful during the busy day, or you didn't get to practice meditation or self-care for the day. Instead of beating yourself up about, try reframing it in a more positive light. You have the gift of tomorrow waiting for you, and you have the power to always try again.

When you feel discouraged, remind yourself why you're doing this. Why did you pick up this book in the first place? Whatever your reason is, there are usually going to be obstacles that'll get in the way trying to drag you down. To overcome these obstacles, create healthy reminders for yourself. If you're thinking: *"I need to change because I hate myself."* Instead, think more positively: *"I'm doing this because I want to make a positive change in myself."*

Like we've discussed before in this book, in the end, we are just people. Nobody gets through this life without a few scrapes and scars along the way. People were born to make mistakes, but if you let your mistakes bog you down each day, it'll cloud your mind and your moods in the long run. You may strive for perfection when in reality perfection can never really be achieved. But don't take this in a negative way. It's more comforting to know that your mistakes are all part of the normal human experience. Even if these "perfect" people did exist, they would certainly have not learned anything during their lives. Those that do believe they're "perfect" also experience great unhappiness that they refuse to acknowledge.

U.S. President Theodore Roosevelt once said, "Comparison is the thief of joy." When you're feeling low, remember that you shouldn't compare yourself to others. Since we're all on the same human path, we each have our struggles and obstacles that we have to deal with at some point in our lives. If you look at someone and think, *"They must have their life together. They seem a lot happier than I am. I'm sure they don't make mistakes like I do."*

Due to the exponential growth of technology, there's been a trend of how the Internet deeply affects your moods. We're able to keep up with people around us through social media. The unfortunate side of this is that those you know are broadcasting the best parts of their lives to the world. When you compare your happiness to their happiness, you fail to recognize them as a human just like you. Behind those smiling faces on the screen, there's a person on the other side that may be going through a difficult time. They may be struggling with an intense battle within themselves, but you would never see that from a photo of them. This is why it's important to always acknowledge people as people, and that includes you.

Our moods are constantly changing, but sometimes they hang on longer than we want them to. If you've been dealing with negative moods for exponential amounts of time, it may be a sign that you need to seek professional help. This may sound scary to you at first. After all, there is often a stigma associated with getting medical help from a therapist. We tend to think that only people with serious conditions need to speak with professionals, or that it's associated with being "crazy." In truth, there is nothing wrong with having to accept outside help, despite this culture of thinking we're deeply broken if we have to rely on therapy.

The purpose of therapy isn't to "cure" you of your negative moods. Instead, there are ways it teaches you how to handle your moods, and how to change them when you're feeling in a bad place. DBT and CBT are specialized forms of therapy that specifically concentrate on moods. They utilize similar practices in this book to help you better understand your moods. In particularly extreme cases of mood-based disorders, such as depression and anxiety, you may need to seek medication that helps balance your brain chemistry to make you feel better. If you think therapy or medication would be beneficial for you and your moods, talk with your doctor to see if these methods are right for you.

Conclusion

By recognizing and growing familiar with changes to your mood, you will put yourself on the successful path of living a fulfilling and happy life. Hopefully, this book has provided some insight into the many ways you can change your mental health for the better. You've already taken the big step of recognizing how you'd like to change, and by utilizing what you've learned from this book you'll be well on your way to changing your moods and feel good about yourself. Even though you get caught up in your daily schedule, if you neglect these helpful tools that shape your moods it can severely and negatively impact your mental health in the future.

Moods seem like they have total control over your thoughts. But ultimately, the choice is up to you with how you handle them. There is always the easy option, the one that encourages you to give up and thrive in negative moods. But following the easy path leads to an unexamined life, a life of never learning anything and always being unhappy. Truly, you are not thriving. It doesn't have to be this way, though. You can reexamine the way you see the world, and use that to shape your moods so that they reflect a more positive way of thinking. Obstacles won't break you. Instead, they'll strengthen you, and you'll even have the energy to ask, *"What's next?"* instead of *"Why me?"*

You now have an understanding of the importance of mindfulness, and how to apply it to your life. Living in the moment can greatly impact your mood, and when you focus on staying in the present, you're more likely to forget about the troubles of your past and ignore the worries of the future. You've learned how important it is to attend to your moods as they arrive because they could have a long-lasting impact on your life if you learn to handle them properly. By examining your thoughts without judgment, you're more likely to gain a better understanding of your moods and how you feel when they're "visiting." Through meditation, you'll be able to recognize your day-to-day moods with ease.

We've also examined how to reframe your thinking when it comes to you and those around you. Through the four pillars covered in this book, you now have a set of guidelines that you can implement in your daily life. By focusing on these pillars, you're more likely to break free from the harmful preconceived patterns of thought that deeply impact your relationships not only with others but with yourself as well. You now know to avoid negative thinking and bad moods by not assuming the worst in people. Through using your words positively, you're more likely to engage in great conversations that leave you feeling good afterward.

It's good to have a healthy balance in your mind, but to feel good it's also important for you to make daily life choices that benefit your physical health as well. Your mental health coincides with how your body feels. If it's feeling bad, then most likely your mind isn't in the best shape as well. Conversely, if you spend ten to thirty minutes a day exercising and getting physical activity, it can greatly improve your mind and your moods. Along with exercise, your diet can also influence how you feel from day-to-day. We've covered how your gut and your mind share a connection, and that by following healthy eating habits you'll be taking steps to feel better. By putting effort into your physical health, you're paving the way for your mental health to improve and eventually thrive to its fullest potential.

With all this focus on mental health, it is understandable to immediately feel overwhelmed or discouraged as you take the leap into changing your moods. The most important thing to remember when changing your moods is that you shouldn't take yourself so seriously. It's a part of life to grow and to change, and it shouldn't be treated as an overwhelming task or something frightening. By loving yourself, and practicing self-compassion, you'll give yourself more confidence to change your life for the better.

Treat yourself the same way you want to treat others, with love and positivity. Speak kind words to yourself, especially when you're frustrated. Write a list of everything you'd like to change about yourself in a positive way, including the unhealthy habits you've done for so long. Make a self-care routine to follow during those times when you just need to rest and repair. If you're still struggling, do not be afraid to reach out and seek help from a support system. It can be a close friend, a family member, and in more difficult cases you can reach out to a doctor or licensed therapist.

Always remember, no matter how positive or negative your moods are, that you are worth it. Strive to try your best, even when your best wasn't as good as it was yesterday. The more you try to recognize and change your moods, the more you'll learn. The more you learn about your moods, the better you will feel. You deserve to be happy, and no bad mood should ever rob you of that joy. Now that you have the tools at your disposal, get out there and reshape yourself to take back your happiness! Turn off that Brain TV and let yourself bask in the beauty of life and the present. Your mind, body, and overall spirit will thank you for taking the time to improve. By reading this book, you're already a few steps ahead!

Change your mind, change your mood, and finally…change your _life_!

Made in the USA
San Bernardino, CA
29 December 2019